# REARING
# RESPONSIBLE
# CHILDREN

# REARING
# RESPONSIBLE
# CHILDREN

*David J. Cherrington*

Library of Congress Catalog Card Number: 97-45344
ISBN 0-8452-2354-5


First edition published by Bookcraft, Inc.,
Salt Lake City, Utah
Second edition published by Brigham Young University,
Provo, Utah 84602


Printed in the United States of America

# *Contents*

Preface

1    Rearing Responsible Children............................1

2    Building Celestial Families ...........................19

3    Effective Child-Rearing Practices....................39

4    Developing Responsibility .............................53

5    Characteristics of Outstanding Workers.........69

6    Teaching Responsibility Through Work.........81

7    Rewarding Good Behavior...........................101

8    Problem-Solving Skills for Parents..............117

9    Discipline Techniques .................................143

10   Parental Influence.......................................167

11   Building Better Relationships ......................185

Notes...................................205

Index .................................211

Author Biography..............................216

# *Preface*

The challenge of rearing responsible children is probably greater today than it has ever been and many parents are seeking help. This book is designed to help parents by providing an easy to read presentation of practical suggestions, examples, theories, and principles. Earlier readers have reported that the ideas presented here helped them understand their responsibilities as parents and gave them the confidence to teach and discipline their children. Interest in the topic of rearing responsible children was demonstrated by the large number of women who attended a session by that title at the BYU Women's Conference, June 1997. About 2,000 women attended the session and another 1,000 were turned away.

The first edition of this book appeared in 1985. This second edition updates some of the research conclusions and contains additional stories illustrating the principles. The greatest change, however, is the addition of chapter 2: Building Celestial Families. This chapter explains how to create stable, happy families and is a significant addition to the book. Many parents have found that these insights regarding celestial behaviors have made a substantial improvement in their families.

This book originated from a research project that began in 1974 and examined the work values of adult employees and the effects of the work ethic on job satisfaction and productivity. The results showed that work values and personal responsibility are largely developed by early child-rearing experiences and the type of discipline and training children receive within the home. From our interviews and questionnaires we concluded that the types of child-rearing practices parents use in the home have an enormous influence on the development of work values and other moral behaviors.

This book presents the major applications of our research and several other studies on moral development. Numerous examples are included to help parents see how these principles can be applied and to demonstrate the kinds of success and failure other parents have experienced. The examples of poor parenting are not meant to criticize, only to illustrate and explain. None of them are entirely real, but neither are they entirely fictitious. They are real in the sense that similar events have occurred, but the names and some of the facts have been changed to provide anonymity. Most of the stories and illustrations are actually composites taken from common experiences of several families.

Three additional resources I highly recommend for parents who are seeking valuable insights in rearing responsible children are *Bringing Up Moral Children* and *Focus on the Children* by A. Lynn Scoresby and *The Seven Habits of Highly Effective Families* by Stephen R. Covey. Scoresby's books explain how parents teach morality and he applies the principles to difficult child-rearing subjects such as sexual morality, self-destructiveness, chemical abuse, respecting authority, and handling money and property. Covey's book is an application of his highly-acclaimed seven habits philosophy to family interactions, and it contains many useful illustrations of what parents and children can do together to build quality family relationships.

# 1

# *Rearing*
# *Responsible Children*

At O'Hare Airport one afternoon I observed one of the nastiest confrontations between a mother and her child that I have ever seen. The child was only two or three years old, but she had a temper that was more vicious than you would expect from a young child. The two hours we spent at the gate seemed like a full afternoon of sheer agony, and after we finally boarded the plane, the two-hour flight seemed to take all night.

While I was sitting in the gate area my reading was interrupted by the loud, angry screaming of the child. In a rage of anger the child demanded a drink of water as she kicked the carry-on baggage and slapped her mother's legs. The mother responded in two totally different ways to her child, and she switched from one to the other as fast as you might change TV channels. At one moment the mother appeared completely calm and controlled as she rationally verbalized the child's feelings. "You're angry with Mommy because she won't let you get a drink. You think Mommy doesn't love you because she doesn't take you to the

water fountain.    You hate Mommy and want to run away."
Suddenly the mother's behavior changed, and in a tone of voice
that was louder than the child's screaming, she scolded and condemned the child.    "Shut up, you little brat; I've had it with you!
I just took you to the water fountain two minutes ago and you
refused to drink."

After ten minutes of screaming, the mother finally gave in and
took the child to the drinking fountain.  When they got there, however, the child refused to drink out of the fountain and demanded
a cup.  Another shouting match ensued, punctuated only by occasional periods when the mother attempted again to verbalize the
child's angry feelings.  "You're angry because Mommy doesn't
have a cup for you."  After several long minutes, one of the passengers went to a refreshment stand and returned with a paper cup.
After filling the cup half full the mother offered the drink to the little tyrant.  "Here's a cup of water, Briton.  That nice gentleman got
you a drink."  The child eyed the cup momentarily, and then threw
it aside on the floor with clenched teeth.

After several more minutes of screaming, another passenger
gave the mother a small sack of M&M candies, hoping the bribe
would pacify the child.  While she ate the first few pieces she
stopped screaming.  But the yelling resumed when she insisted
on holding the entire sack of candy.  After several minutes of
protesting the mother finally gave in and handed the child the
remainder of the sack.  Almost immediately the child scattered
the candy on the floor and continued her temper tantrum.   I
assumed this behavior had been going on all day and was
amazed that either of them had the energy or the voice to continue screaming as they did.

The only pause occurred shortly after we boarded the plane,
when one of the flight attendants spent a few minutes visiting
with the child and blowing up a balloon for her.  The person sitting by them asked to be moved as soon as the seat belt sign was
turned off, and other passengers nearby looked as if they, too,
wanted to be moved.  When the meal was served the child insist-

ed on eating the dessert first. The mother tried with only limited success to get the child to eat something else besides the dessert. The child screamed in protest and ultimately succeeded in dumping most of the food on the floor. Every few minutes throughout most of the flight the angry screams of the child rang through the airplane, and the mother proclaimed in words just as loud, "Oh, you little brat, I hate you. I'm going to get rid of you. Shut up and hold still!"

At one point in the flight the child succeeded in getting the mother to take her to the restroom. As I reached out to steady the child as she was dragging her mother down the aisle, the mother looked at me, rolled her eyes, and asked, "Is this how raising children is supposed to be?" For three hours I had been thinking of advice to give, but when I was asked, all I said was "Sometimes it's pretty difficult."

I wish I had another opportunity to answer this mother's question. No, this is definitely not the way raising children is supposed to be. If a child has learned to be so belligerent and disrespectful by the age of three, it frightens me to think what she will be like at age ten or fifteen. I fear that this mother will have many unhappy years of disappointment and frustration.

This mother's child-rearing problem did not start at the airport. What happened at the airport only illustrated an ongoing pattern of inadequate discipline. The child had not learned respect for the authority of parents nor had she learned to accept restraint.

A public airport is not a convenient place for parents to discipline children or to establish their authority as parents. These lessons should have been learned at home through earlier parent-child encounters. Every parent has probably faced the embarrassment of having children misbehave in public—temper tantrums in front of 100 onlookers are never easy to handle. But occasional difficulties are quite different than the history of ineffective parenting demonstrated by this mother.

## Is This How Raising Children Is Supposed to Be?

Parents who are the most successful at raising happy, well-behaved, and socially responsible children are actively involved in their children's lives. They are effective leaders and managers in their homes. They have clear standards of right and wrong and very strict expectations about how their children should behave. Their discipline is firm but loving. They are strong active leaders who teach their children how they should live and why responsible behavior is important; and they demonstrate it by their own example. They manage the affairs of the home by planning meaningful family activities, organizing the work so everything gets done, and motivating family members to cooperatively and enthusiastically work together.

As you observe families in any neighborhood, you find significant differences in the quality of family life and the social responsibility of the children. These differences are primarily created by different child-rearing practices. Most contrasts between effective and ineffective parenting are not as dramatic as the following story illustrates, but the consequences of parenting are profound.

The Johnson family lived in a large frame house with the fruit shed behind it. They moved two years ago and no one was sad to see them leave. Their children were the most disrespectful, belligerent, and uncooperative children in the neighborhood. Every neighbor had a collection of stories about the escapades of the Johnson children, and although the stories became a little exaggerated, they were basically true.

The oldest son, Robert, was twenty when the Johnsons moved. He had graduated from high school, but everyone knew it was simply because the teachers didn't want him back another year. He had clearly not met the graduation requirements because he failed several classes and ran away from home for over half of his sophomore year. At seventeen he was nicknamed "Big Bad Bob" because of his reckless driving and disregard for the law. One night he tried to outrun the police to avoid a speeding ticket.

But in trying to break through a police blockade he destroyed both the family car and a police vehicle. For a while his mother thought the accident would have a good effect on him. In the hospital he told her he was sorry for what he had done, and for the first time in many years he told her he loved her. When he was back on his feet, however, he began once again driving recklessly—this time, however, without a driver's license or permission to use the new family car. When he was eighteen his nickname was changed to "Burnout Bob" because of his drug habits.

The second child, Lisa, was almost seventeen when the family moved, but she very seldom stayed at home. She was generally considered a good student and had remarkably good grades until her junior year in high school. She developed an interest in boys at a very early age, and admitted she was sexually active at the age of fourteen. During the summer when she was fifteen, she spent two months traveling with an older, divorced man in his camper. Her mother's efforts to caution her about her behavior led to an antagonistic relationship. Lisa refused to speak to her mother; even simple comments such as "Hello" and "How are you?" were ignored.

The third child, thirteen-year-old Andy, was remembered for his vicious pranks and meanness. No one knew for sure whether all of the stories they heard about how he tortured stray cats and dogs were true, but some of the stories could be documented, and there were certainly not as many stray cats and dogs anymore. Andy was responsible for burning the old tool shed when he was playing with firecrackers. Because of his vicious and cruel temper, other neighborhood boys usually avoided him, and he did not have any close friends.

Linda was only two years younger than Andy, and much of his nasty temperament had rubbed off on her. When playing with younger children, Linda was domineering and spiteful. Because of her ferocious temper, none of the younger children in the neighborhood were willing to be around her, either. When she was with adults her behavior was entirely different; she behaved so shyly and uncomfortably that very few adults could ever get her to talk with them. She was generally too shy to even answer simple questions such as "How are you doing in school?"

The fifth child, Karen, protected herself from other family members by developing a very loud and foul mouth. Her memory seemed to grasp every foul word and profane comment she ever heard and to store them away for future use. When she was only three or four, some people thought it was cute to see such a colorful vocabulary in a young child. But before she left the neighborhood at the age of nine she could intimidate anyone by stringing together a unique combination of the most vile and filthy words.

The baby of the family was known in the neighborhood as the "Whiner." From the time he was born until the age of seven he spent most of his time crying. The neighbors said they could always tell when the Johnson kids were outside playing because they could hear Brandon whining and crying. He seemed to cry about everything—because he either had been hurt, he expected to be hurt, or he was being ignored. The only time he wasn't crying was when he was playing with children in another yard. Other mothers refused to let him play in their yard unless he stopped crying.

The parents felt very frustrated and defeated by their family situation. Neither of them enjoyed spending time with the children, and they usually tried to avoid being together as a family. Mr. Johnson was an iron worker, both by profession and by avocation. When he came home from work he usually went out to the fruit shed to make wrought-iron fences or window shutters. He was very disappointed in his children and usually tried to avoid talking about them. "I've worked hard all my life for my children so I could give them what they wanted. Kids have to have the freedom to grow up and learn to take care of themselves. You can't fence them in and tie them down like animals. Sometimes they don't do everything they are supposed to do, but if you give them the time and freedom, pretty soon they come around."

Mrs. Johnson thought she had been a good mother when her children were younger. All she had to do then was feed them, bathe them, change them, and rock them to sleep. When her oldest children became teenagers, however, she realized she was not coping very well. The family no longer ate together, and the house was disorganized. The kitchen was continually filled with dirty dishes, and the bedrooms, bathrooms, and laundry room were filled with dirty clothes lying all over the floor. Mrs. Johnson felt particularly defeated by Lisa's refusal to talk to her. Life inside the home was constantly filled with fighting, complaining, and criticism. Mrs. Johnson's efforts to clean the house and prepare food were inadequate and unappreciated. She admitted that the only contentment and satisfaction she found in life was watching television. The soap operas and other TV programs created a fantasy life free of fighting and complaining within her own family. Mr. and Mrs. Johnson did not enjoy being parents. Both of them looked forward to the day when their children would be gone from home and on their own.

While they lived in the neighborhood, many of the neighbors were generously kind to the Johnsons in their comments: "Well, they lived in that old run-down farmhouse, and the place was just too large to really care for. The fruit shed was falling apart, and with all of that old equipment lying around the yard, anyone would be depressed." "They were really caught in a bad situation; maybe this move was the best thing that could happen to them." After the Johnson family moved, however, the new owners made many of the neighbors question their "run-down farm" excuse.

The Johnson house was purchased by the Hansen family, who also had six children—the oldest had just graduated from high school, the youngest was just four. After the furniture was moved in and settled, the Hansen family began to systematically transform their home from a two-acre junk lot into an attractive residence. The weeds were cut and burned, fences were repaired, old machinery was either sold for antiques or repaired and restored, and a new roof was put on the fruit shed. The fruit trees that were still alive were pruned and cared for, and some of the dead fruit trees were replaced.

The fruit shed was no longer needed to store fruit, so the children used it for their hobbies. One of the girls used one corner as a place for her pet rabbits. In another corner one of the boys built cages to house his homing pigeons. Most of the shed, however, was used as a chicken coop, which served as a family project. Every family member participated in the chicken project by either feeding and caring for the chickens, cleaning the coop, gathering the eggs, washing the eggs, or selling them in the neighborhood. The family garden was another family project that involved everyone part time during the summer months.

All but the youngest child had learned to play the piano, and the four older children also played a musical instrument in the school band. At a neighborhood Christmas party the family organized a family band and performed a medley of Christmas carols. All of the children appeared to be happy, outgoing, and friendly individuals. Each family member displayed a strong sense of loyalty to the family. They spent time together and looked forward with great anticipation to family vacations, outings, and family projects.

The happiness that filled the Hansen home did not go unnoticed by other neighbors. When the Hansen family arrived, the whole neighborhood changed. Other parents wanted to have their children play with the Hansen children and work with them on their family projects.

The contrast between the Johnson family and the Hansen family was such a stark contrast that no one in the neighborhood failed to notice it. While one family was falling apart and creating misery, unhappiness, and illegal behavior, the other family was producing happy, productive, and well-behaved children. Although this contrast is rather extreme, almost every neighborhood has families similar to the Johnsons and the Hansens.

What causes such dramatic differences between families? Why are the children in some families having trouble with drugs, alcohol, teenage pregnancies, dismissal from school, and reckless driving convictions, while the children in other families are performing well in school, developing their musical talents, and enthusiastically participating in family projects and work assignments?

The major differences lie in the family environments and child-rearing practices of the parents. Some parents think heredity plays a significant role in explaining such differences. But heredity has very little to do with the variables that create socially responsible children. The genes a child brings into this world may play an important role in determining his height, hair color, and coordination, but not whether he smokes marijuana, tries to outrun the police, or uses foul language. These personal behaviors and characteristics are determined primarily by family characteristics, by the influence of parents, and by the kind of discipline and love found within the home.

## What Does It Mean To Teach Responsibility To Children?

Raising children is not an easy task. When they are small you don't expect them to do much. But as they grow older you expect them to care for themselves and to help with family chores. A five-year-old ought to be able to pick up her own toys after she is through playing. An eight-year-old ought to be able to make her own bed every morning. And if a twelve-year-old can't pick up his dirty clothes from his bedroom floor and put them in the dirty-clothes hamper, he shouldn't complain when his favorite T-shirt isn't washed and ready to wear.

Most parents agree that children should be expected to perform family chores and help the family when they are old enough to do so. As soon as they are physically capable, most parents believe children should be expected to set the table, wash the dishes, clean the house, work in the yard, or perform other family chores. Most parents agree that it is reasonable to expect children to help—they should be responsible for doing their share.

Teaching children responsibility is more than getting children to do their share of the work. It is even more than getting them to consistently pick up their wet towel. A group of parents who have been highly successful in raising healthy and socially responsible children was asked to explain what it means to them to teach responsibility to children. They offered these definitions:

- Becoming responsible means developing positive work values, moral behaviors, and social responsibility.
- Being responsible requires the development of character. It involves teaching our children to be dependable—that fulfilling commitments and keeping promises is more important than doing what they want to do at the moment.
- Becoming responsible is accomplishing the purpose of mortality. Our test in this life is to see if we will be obedient to God and have enough faith and commitment to make the right choices so we can return to Him.
- Becoming responsible is being mature, reliable, helpful, independent, and a self-starter. It is also being honest, trustworthy, and socially aware. If children are only responsible when someone else is watching, or only when being paid, or simply to impress others, it hasn't become part of their character and it won't stick.
- Being responsible is becoming mature in the sense of being responsible to family, to self, to god and to others.

## What is My Responsibility?

Raising children ought to be an exhilarating, exciting, and pleasant experience. Parents should think their children are their best friends—there are no finer people on earth with whom they would rather spend time visiting, sharing life's experiences, confiding feelings, or going on vacations. Ideally, family relationships should create the strongest social ties in an individual's life. When family relationships are positive and uplifting, parents and children develop a bond of friendship based on mutual love, respect, and admiration.

Unfortunately, the family relationships in many families leave much to be desired.  Rather than thinking of their children as their best friends, many parents regard them as their most ardent critics; and many children see their parents as public enemy number one.

Parents and children need to respect one another as unique individuals  who have genuine feelings and interests.  Children need to have confidence in their parents' ability to teach and guide them, and parents need to have confidence in their children's ability to grow and develop.  Both parents and children need to trust one another, and each needs to have confidence that the other will make good decisions and exercise good judgment.  Parents and children should also love and admire one another.  These four characteristics—*respect, confidence, trust, and love*—need to be cultivated in every relationship between parents and children.

Every family falls short of this ideal in some way or another.  Even the best families have some bad days.  Although good parents usually feel pleased with their family and are proud of their children's progress, some days they think things are really falling apart.  Occasionally, every family is required to muddle through conflict and bad feelings as part of the development process.  Even solid, happy families experience times when conflicts have to be resolved, schedules have to be coordinated, and hurt feelings need to be discussed.  Good family relationships don't just happen; they are created with a lot of effort over an extended period of time.  Chapter 2 describes the foundation principles for creating happy and healthy families.

When family relationship's  are toxic and sour, everyone is unhappy and miserable—both parents and children.  The bad feelings didn't occur all at once, and the conditions that created the conflict did not arise overnight.  When bad relationships exist, the parents may feel the situation is out of control and begin to ask, "What is our responsibility and how can we get out of this now?"  The responsibilities of parents can be examined from three perspectives:  legal, social, and moral.

***Legal responsibility***.  The legal responsibilities of parents in caring for their children are rather limited relative to how extensively other aspects of social life have been legislated. But the legal responsibilities are expanding because some parents are unwilling to accept their obligations as parents and others are negligent.

Until they are 18 years of age, parents are required to provide the basic necessities for their children and protect their interests. If they fail to provide adequate protection and care, the children can be taken by the state and placed in foster homes. They can also be placed in foster care is there is evidence of parental abuse, either physical or sexual. Parents are required to co-sign before children can obtain certain privileges such as borrowing money and receiving a driver's license. If the child defaults on the loan or has an auto accident, the parents are financially responsible. Parents have the responsibility to represent their children and protect their interests, such as authorizing their participation in intrusive psychological studies or medical procedures including surgeries and body piercing.

Parents also have a legal responsibility to ensure their children obtain an education. Although they have considerable latitude in choosing between public schools, private schools, or home education, and they also have some discretion in selecting the content of what they want their children learn, they have a responsibility to make certain their children are educated. Children are required to attend school and parents have a responsibility to make certain they are there.

Because of the alarming increase in juvenile delinquency, juvenile judges have tried some creative approaches to reduce teenage truancy and crime by holding parents more responsible for their children's misbehavior. Some parents have been required to attend school with their children. Other parents have been required to perform community service with their children. One mother who complained that she could not control her daughter's actions was handcuffed to her daughter. Efforts have been made to hold parents liable for their children's drinking when the alcohol was obtained at home and contributed to an auto accident.

Couples are required to obtain a marriage license before they get married; but they are not required to get married to have children, nor are they required to obtain a permit to give birth to a child. Parents don't even have to pass certification requirements to show they are either competent or adequately trained to rear a child. In fact, our society seems more concerned about legislating the distribution of birth control devices and allowing abortions on demand than in requiring parents to properly raise their children. The world is more concerned with preventing life and taking life than with giving life and making it more abundant.

*Social responsibility.* Parent's social responsibilities in raising their children change over time and vary from culture to culture. In middle-class America, most parents assume a financial responsibility for their children until they reach the age of eighteen and are out of high school. Young adults who pursue their education beyond high school may receive financial aid from their parents, but many college students are expected to support themselves, even if they come from financially wealthy homes.

The responsibility for teaching social values has shifted significantly over the last century from the home to society. Children spend a considerably larger portion of their time in schools now than did children a hundred years ago, and many parents believe the schools are responsible for teaching social values. Most parents, of course, are not willing to admit it, but a careful analysis of what they fail to teach in the home shows how seriously they have abdicated their responsibility to the schools.

In other cultures the responsibilities of parents are significantly different than in the United States. In the Asian cultures of Japan and China, parent-child relationships persist relatively unchanged throughout the lives of both. Children are expected to obey and show respect to their parents regardless of their age. Even adults in their fifties and sixties are still expected to show obedience and respect to their parents as long as they live. In these cultures, children of all ages are expected to seek advice from their parents regarding financial dealings, household activities, and personal concerns.

While American parents tend to kick their children out of the nest and expect them to fly on their own at the age of eighteen, most Arab families assume a financial and social responsibility that extends well beyond the age of eighteen and is not limited to just the core family. A twenty-five-year-old student who has done well in college may expect financial assistance from uncles and other distant relatives to help him obtain a medical degree. If a thirty-five-year-old decides to start a business, he would turn first to the extended family to help him secure venture capital.

***Moral responsibility.*** Parents have a moral responsibility to teach and train their children that goes beyond the norms of society. Although the percentage of parents who feel this way has declined over the past century, many parents still believe they have a moral obligation to teach their children social values and provide for them financially. The basis for this moral value stems from a religious belief and is clearly explained in the following scriptures.

> And these words, which I command thee this day, shall be in thine heart: And thou shalt teach them diligently unto thy children, and shalt talk of them when thou sittest in thine house, and when thou walkest by the way, and when thou liest down, and when thou risest up. (Deuteronomy 6:6, 7.)
>
> He that spareth his rod hateth his son: but he that loveth him chasteneth him betimes (Proverbs 13:24.)
>
> Train up a child in the way he should go: and when he is old, he will not depart from it. (Proverbs 22: 6.)
>
> But if any provide not for his own, and specially for those of his own house, he hath denied the faith, and is worse than an infidel. (1 Timothy 5:8.)
>
> And ye will not suffer your children that they go hungry, or naked; neither will ye suffer that they transgress the laws of God, and fight and quarrel one with another, and serve the devil. . . . But ye will teach them to walk in the ways of truth and soberness; ye will teach them to love one another, and to serve one another. (Mosiah 4:14, 15).
>
> And again, inasmuch as parents have children in Zion, or in any

of her stakes which are organized, that teach them not to understand the doctrine of repentance, faith in Christ the son of the living God, and of baptism and the gift of the Holy Ghost by the laying on of the hands, when eight years old, the sin be upon the heads of the parents. . . . And they shall also teach their children to pray, and to walk uprightly before the Lord. (Doctrine and Covenants 68:25, 28.)

An interesting biblical story that emphasizes the importance of parents teaching their children is contained in the first book of Samuel, chapters 2 through 4. The prophet Eli had two sons who were guilty of sexual transgressions and desecrating the sacrifices. Eli attempted to chastise his sons for their iniquity, but they would not listen to their father. Eli apparently thought he could offer sacrifices to atone for the errors of his sons, but the Lord refused to accept Eli's offering. Instead, the Lord condemned both Eli and his sons because of the sons' wickedness and Eli's failure to restrain them (see 1 Samuel 3:11-14).

## It's Never Too Late to Start

The first four or five years of a child's life are a critical period when the child can be taught proper attitudes and values. These early concepts become rather permanent. When the opportunity of those years is past, however, the child will never be as receptive again. Parents who fail to help their children develop self-discipline and self-control during those early years face a difficult uphill battle as they attempt to correct problems in later years.

Regardless of how seriously they failed in the early years, however, parents should never give up or assume it is too late to improve the relationship. It is never too late to start.

A twenty-four-year-old woman who was working as a counselor in an alcohol and drug prevention center told me the following personal story. When she was a child her parents were extremely lenient and permissive, allowing her to grow up as an irresponsible and unrestrained youngster. As a teenager she failed most of her classes in junior high school, and she finally dropped out of school in her sophomore year. Her parents gave her everything she ever wanted, hoping to buy her cooperation.

Perhaps the greatest sacrifice they made was to sell their home and move to another side of town, hoping she would attend a different high school. The choir in the new high school had planned a trip to Europe, and the parents thought that if they could get their daughter into this school she would be motivated by the opportunity of traveling in Europe with the choir. The parents' plan failed, however, because their daughter did not stay in school.

When she turned sixteen, the parents tried once again to buy her cooperation by letting her have a birthday party with her friends. During the first two hours of the party the parents watched in horror as their daughter's unruly friends stained the carpet, destroyed the furniture, and scattered a mess throughout the house. In sheer disgust, the parents finally sent the girl to her room and told her friends to leave. While the father was sending the friends away, the mother went to her daughter's room to talk with her. When the father returned a few minutes later, he found his wife lying on the floor with blood dripping from her forehead. The daughter had struck her mother with a baton and left the house through the back door.

This violent confrontation helped the parents realize the mistake they had made in trying to give their daughter everything she wanted. On many earlier occasions they had faced the despair of not knowing what to do to correct their earlier mistakes. They did not want their daughter to run away from home, and their goal had been to do everything they could to avoid conflict, hoping that when she was a little older she would behave more responsibly. However, this approach had not worked, and they regretted that they could not go back now to correct their mistakes.

When the daughter returned home two days later, the parents had a carefully and firmly planned approach for handling this problem. The father insisted that his daughter sit down and listen to him. She did not want to talk and attempted to leave. He physically restrained her and told her that he was going to tie her to the chair if necessary until she heard what he had to say. Realizing that she had little choice, she listened defiantly to what he said. The father explained that she would no longer be treated as a member of the family. They did not want her running away and she was welcome to live at home, but in the future she would live in the home as a guest. Her status as a guest was explained in only general terms. She would be neither asked nor allowed to assist in any family responsibilities—preparing the food, cleaning the house, or even making her own bed. Her bedroom would no longer be her bedroom but would now be a guest bedroom that she would be invited to use. On all future family activities, she would only be invited to participate as a guest. She would not be considered part of the family.

The father's lecture was as puzzling to the daughter as it was surprising. At first she expected to be whipped or punished in some physical way. It didn't make any sense to hear her father tell her that she would no longer be required or even allowed to do jobs around the home. If she wasn't allowed to make her bed or clean her room, who would do it?

When she looked at her bedroom the change was obvious. All of her posters had been removed and the walls had been repainted. Many of the things she had kept in her dresser drawers had been removed, and the items that remained were rearranged and reorganized. Likewise, her closet had been cleaned, and while most of her clothes were still there, they were arranged quite differently. Immodest and indecent clothing had been removed. She was told that her bed would be made every day and changed twice a week, and that all of her dirty clothes would be picked up, laundered, and returned. Her parents and two younger brothers treated her politely and with respect, but with a cool detachment, emphasizing her status as an outsider.

At first she thought this change was absurd. She didn't have to help with the dishes; she didn't have to make her own bed; she didn't have to do any of the family chores. But the reality of being an outsider rather than an integral member of the family unit soon became very painful. After several months she began cleaning her room and making her own bed in spite of her parents' protests. It was almost a year later before she asked her parents if she could once again become a member of the family. She had tried feebly on several occasions to begin doing other family chores, and each time her parents told her not to do it but to spend more time thinking about it. She cried with joy when her father finally told her that she was welcome to become a member of the family again and invited her to do her share of the housework.

The father's approach in this situation had a very profound influence on the behavior of his daughter. Problems continued to occur, and some of them were not very adequately resolved, but the relationship between parents and daughter had at least made a significant turn and was once again going uphill, even though the hill was a bit bumpy. The responsibility of parents does not end at age six when children begin school, nor at age eighteen when they finish school. Parents always have a responsibility to their children, and children always have a responsibility to their parents. Regardless of how bad the relationship has been in the past, neither parents nor children should assume that a relationship is hopeless. It is never too late to begin improving a relationship.

## Summary

*A healthy family environment helps children become socially responsible and well-behaved.*

*Parents have a legal, social, and moral responsibility to raise responsible children: "And they shall teach their children to pray, and to walk uprightly before the Lord" (D&C 68:28).*

*Regardless of how defiant and rebellious a child may be, parents should not abandon hope or stop trying. It is never too late to change.*

# 2

# *Building Celestial Families*

How would you describe your family environment? Is it a home filled with anger and hostility? Is it a home where members live their lives independently but peacefully? Or is it a happy and supportive home? Whatever it is, it has a significant influence on the character development of both parents and children. This chapter describes three very different levels of living and explains why most family environments are less than ideal.

Healthy families tend to produce responsible children, while dysfunctional families tend to produce dysfunctional children. Perhaps the greatest challenge for parents is to create a stable, supportive, and righteous family environment for their children. The influence of such an environment on children is almost too great and enduring to describe. Although teenagers are influenced by many forces outside the family, their family environment continues to have a sizable influence on them because of parental expectations and the value framework they acquired earlier.

Happy and healthy families don't just happen by chance. People are very fortunate if they belong to a supportive family that provides love and encouragement; but these conditions are not created by luck or chance. The basic principles for creating quality family environments are summarized in a Proclamation to the World:

"Happiness in family life is most likely to be achieved when founded upon the teachings of the Lord Jesus Christ. Successful marriages and families are established and maintained on principles of faith, prayer, repentance, forgiveness, respect, love, compassion, work and wholesome recreational activities." [1]

Happiness in all families, Christian or non-Christian, depends on following correct principles as taught by the Savior.

## Three Levels of Living

A father made the following comment: "The quality of our family life changed dramatically after I learned about celestial, terrestrial, and telestial behavior.[2] I always thought these were the three degrees of glory in the life hereafter and they didn't apply to this life. But then I discovered they also apply to how we behave in this life. I decided to start acting a little more celestially. It wasn't easy and I'm still not perfect. But I know from personal experience that the change in my behavior made an enormous difference in our family."

Our day to day behavior can be classified into one of three major categories based on scriptural references that describe the three degrees of glory in the life hereafter. These scriptures explain that there are three significantly different levels of living: *(1) telestial behavior, (2) terrestrial behavior, and (3) celestial behavior.*[3] Our moral conduct — what we do and say and how we treat others — can generally be placed in one of these three categories and we are free to decide what our behavior will be. How we choose to respond determines the kind of life we live;

and our choices determine the quality of family life for ourselves and other family members.

## 1.  Telestial Behavior

A telestial way of living is followed by those who disregard and resist the commandments of God and the laws of society. They seek to pursue their own interests and walk in their own way. The attributes of telestial people are described as follows:[4]

"These are they who received not the gospel of Christ, neither the testimony of Jesus."

"These are they who are liars, and sorcerers, and adulterers, and whoremongers, and whosoever loves and makes a lie."

"These are they who suffer the wrath of God on earth." (D&C 76:82, 103, 104)

So what are Telestial people like?  What kind of attitudes, motives, and communication patterns are characteristic of Telestial people?

- These people are self-centered; they are only concerned about their own selfish interests and lustful desires.  Liars and sorcerers are people who use deception for their own benefit. Adulterers and whoremongers pursue sexual gratifications for their personal pleasures.
- These are the people who ask "What's in it for me?  Is this fun and pleasurable?"  Their goal is to take the easy route and do whatever seems expedient.
- These are people who are unwilling to accept accountability or responsibility for their selfish actions. They do not keep covenants or live true to the commitments they make.

## 2.  Terrestrial Behavior

Terrestrial living is an honorable way of life that is based on following the social customs and cultural norms of society. This way of life is offered by society through rational learning, legal legislation, social organizations, and religious    institutions. Terrestrial people are described as people who died without law or who rejected the testimony of Jesus in mortality. They are also described as the "honorable men of the earth, who were blinded by the craftiness of men."[5] Alvin R. Dyer said of this group: "These, for the most part, will be men who, during earth-life existence, sought the excellence of men; and some who gave of their time and talents and endeavor to the ways of manmade ideals of culture, science, and education, but thought not to include God and his ways in their search for a complete life."[6]

Terrestrial people are also those who were "not valiant in the testimony of Jesus."[7] Spencer W. Kimball commented on this verse: "I wish our Latter-day Saints could become more valiant. As I read the seventy-sixth section of the Doctrine and Covenants, the great vision given to the Prophet Joseph Smith, I remember that the Lord says to that terrestrial degree of glory may go those who are not valiant in the testimony, which means that many of us who have received baptism by proper authority, many who have received other ordinances, even temple blessings, will not reach the celestial kingdom of glory unless we live the commandments and are valiant."[8]

What are the attributes of terrestrial people?

- They are good people who want to make laws and live by them.
- They accept social conventions and try to uphold them.
- They want to live in peace and expect everyone to do their part.
- They are honorable people who accept the norm of reciprocity and want to do what is just and fair.

Terrestrial people are good people. It is probably true that for many of us we are living a terrestrial life when we are at our best. A friend once suggested that we form a "Shoot for Terrestrial" club.

### 3. Celestial Behavior

Celestial living is the way of life followed by those who earnestly seek to adhere to the eternal truths revealed by God. The attributes of celestial living are briefly described in the following verses:[9]

"These are they who received the testimony of Jesus, and believed on his name and were baptized after the manner of his burial..."

"That by keeping the commandments they might be washed and cleansed from all their sins and receive the Holy Spirit..."

"And who overcome by faith and are sealed by the Holy Spirit of promise, which the Father sheds forth upon all those who are just and true."

"And they shall overcome all things."

"These are they who are just men made perfect through Jesus the mediator of the new covenant..."

"...and they see as they are seen, and know as they are known,..."  (D&C 76:51–53, 60, 69, 94)

What are Celestial people like?  These are people:
* who *receive the gospel of Jesus*,
* who are *valiant in the testimony of Jesus*,
* who are *just and true*, and
* who *overcome all things*.

In other words, these are people who follow Christ's pattern for living.  What does it mean to be "just and true," or to be "valiant in the testimony of Jesus?"  How did the Savior teach us to live?

# Christ's Pattern for Living

One of the best places to find Christ's pattern of living is in the Sermon on the Mount —Matthew 5-7.  Jesus probably repeated this great sermon time after time as he taught in the synagogues

of the northern Galilean cities of Israel during the first 18 months
of his ministry. He repeated it again to the people in America after
his resurrection.[10] This great sermon provides the foundation for
couples to create a happy marriage and for parents to raise responsible children. The beatitudes contain a summary of celestial attitudes and behaviors.[11]

- "Blessed are the poor in spirit." To be poor in spirit means to
  be humble and teachable. It means not being arrogant or self-
  centered. It means not being so self-assured that we are
  unwilling to consider the interests and ideas of others.
- "Blessed are they that mourn." People who mourn are those
  who feel a genuine sorrow for their own mistakes and an
  empathetic sadness for the pains and anguish of others. This
  does not mean that we should be constantly sad and morose;
  indeed, we should be happy and cheerful. But we should feel
  genuine remorse or sorrow at appropriate times.
- "Blessed are the meek." To be meek means to be patient and
  mild, not inclined to anger or resentment. Someone who is
  meek would not have a "short fuse" or "buttons that are easily pushed." Nor would they be described as someone who
  "flies off the handle quickly" or who "bites off someone's
  head."
- "Blessed are all they who do hunger and thirst after righteousness." To be righteous means to be moral and ethical —
  to be morally justifiable and fair. Those who hunger and thirst
  after righteousness are those who seek to know what is morally right and how they ought to live. They strive to live a vir-
  tuous life in an upright manner. And the promise is that they
  shall be filled with the Holy Ghost, whose role in the Godhead
  is to reveal truth and wisdom.
- "Blessed are the merciful." Mercy means kindness, forbearance,
  and compassion. To show mercy means to refrain from harming
  or punishing offenders; it involves showing kindness beyond
  what may be expected or demanded by the rules of fairness.
- "Blessed are the pure in heart." The pure in heart are those

whose appetites, passions, and desires are purged of evil and sin. To have a pure heart means to have pure motives and to seek for goodness and kindness.

- "Blessed are the peacemakers." Peacemakers are not just those who intervene in disputes, but also those who demonstrate in their lives a spirit of contentment, cooperation, and peace. The physical presence of peacemakers can change the dynamics of a group and motivate members to pursue cooperative solutions where everyone wins rather than conflict solutions where someone wins at the expense of others.
- "Blessed are they which are persecuted for righteousness' sake." We should stand for truth and righteousness and seek to encourage honor and virtue. Being valiant in the testimony of Jesus requires us to be steady and unwavering at all times and not just when it is convenient or socially acceptable.
- "Blessed are ye when men shall revile you and persecute you, and shall say all manner of evil against you falsely for my sake. Rejoice, and be exceeding glad: for great is your reward in heaven: for so persecuted they the prophets which were before you."

In the Sermon on the Mount, Jesus taught his disciples how to live a higher, celestial law than the terrestrial Law of Moses they had been living. While the Law of Moses taught "Thou shalt not kill," Jesus declared in the Sermon on the Mount that we should not even get angry: "Whosoever is angry with his brother without a cause shall be in danger of the judgment...whosoever shall say, Thou fool, shall be in danger of hell fire."[12]

While the Law of Moses commanded "Thou shalt not commit adultery," Jesus declared in the Sermon on the Mount that we should control our lustful desires: "Whosoever looketh on a woman to lust after her hath committed adultery with her already in his heart."[13]

While the Law of Moses commanded us to avoid using the name of deity in vain, Jesus taught that we should be circumspect in all our conversations. Our communications should be simple and respectful; we should respond with simple comments of yes and no rather than "For heaven's sake, yes!" or "Hell, no!"

The Law of Moses advocated the norm of reciprocity: an eye for an eye and a tooth for a tooth. But Jesus taught his hearers to turn the other cheek, to go the second mile, and to love their enemies: "Whosoever shall smite thee on the right cheek, turn to him the other also. And if any man will sue thee at the law, and take away thy coat, let him have thy cloak also. And whosoever shall compel thee to go a mile, go with him twain. Give to him that asketh thee and from him that would borrow of thee turn not thou away. Ye have heard that it hath been said, Thou shalt love thy neighbour, and hate thine enemy. But I say unto you, Love your enemies, bless them that curse you, do good to them that hate you, and pray for them which despitefully use you, and persecute you."[14]

## Everyday Terrestrial Living

Unfortunately, most of our everyday behaviors are below the celestial standards taught in the Sermon on the Mount. Even when we think we are good, we are usually just terrestrial. To the extent that we avoid being selfish or cruel, we rise above telestial living. But, how often do we rise above terrestrial living? Terrestrial family environments can be peaceful when everyone follows the family's rules, but these conditions do not inspire nobility of character or provide the best foundation for moral development.

Parents should examine their behavior and assess how they treat each other and their children. If they want to have celestial homes, they need to act celestially. Most families probably have more terrestrial than celestial behaviors. How familiar do the following statements sound? These statements come from young married couples who were describing their accommodation to marriage.

1. I fixed the meal so you should wash the dishes.
2. I'll rub your back for five minutes if you'll rub mine for five minutes.

3. I changed the baby's diaper last time; its your turn this time.
4. We visited your home last Thanksgiving so its only fair that we visit my home this year.
5. We have an agreement that if I do the laundry she cleans the apartment.
6. She criticized my mother's cooking so I told her what I thought about her dad's driving.
7. We have a very well-organized home: I fix dinner Monday, Wednesday, and Friday and she fixes dinner Tuesday, Thursday and Sunday. The one who fixes the meal has to clean the kitchen. I fix my own breakfast and she drinks that instant junk. I eat lunch on campus and Saturday night is our date night. On Sunday and Monday night I watch football and she gets to watch her dumb sit-coms Tuesday, Wednesday, and Thursday nights. I wash her car if she irons my shirts.

The last comment was made by a husband who claimed he had the most organized and stable marriage of anyone he knew. For the most part, these rules sound reasonable and fair. Rules like these are often viewed as necessary for creating an organized family life. They are also consistent with the law of reciprocity, which says I have an obligation to help others in exchange for them helping me.

But, none of these statements describe celestial reactions. Following terrestrial rules that are fair and equal is certainly much better than self-centered telestial behavior. But living by fair rules and abiding by the law of reciprocity is less than celestial living. To paraphrase the Savior, don't the Scribes and Pharisees also do this!

If these rules sound like a Pharisaic Code, we ought to remember what Christ said about the Pharisees and Scribes. "For I say unto you, that except your righteousness shall exceed the righteousness of the Scribes and Pharisees, ye shall in no case enter into the kingdom of heaven."[15]

In many ways, the Scribes and Pharisees were the good people at the time of Christ. "Pharisee" comes from the Hebrew: Perushim, meaning "separated," which was the same as the Assideans, which meant "godly men" or "saints". The Pharisees prided themselves on their strict observance of the law. Their teachings tended to reduce religious life to the observance of a multiplicity of ceremonial rules and to encourage self-sufficiency and spiritual pride. Nevertheless, the Pharisees and Scribes were not living a celestial life and the Savior condemned them for hypocrisy.

How do we apply these levels of living in our homes to create happy families? Building a celestial family requires that family members behave celestially. Telestial behaviors destroy relationships and create unhappy families. Terrestrial behaviors allow family members to live together in peace; but they don't establish really happy families. If families want to be happy, they need to learn how to display celestial behaviors.

## Family Applications

Recognizing the differences between celestial, terrestrial, and telestial behaviors was a valuable first step toward greater family happiness in our family. After we discussed the differences, some family members started to use them to label the conduct of other family members. On one occasion, for example, one of the boys ate the remainder of a cake rather than share it with the other children. Obviously, this was unfair and one of the girls reprimanded him by saying "That was certainly very telestial of you to eat all the cake!" He replied, "Well, it was certainly very terrestrial of you to criticize me." Labeling our behavior in this way helped us discover how often our behavior was not as good as it should have been.

An event in our home helped us understand more clearly the differences between these three motives. At that time we had a dish washing schedule that required each child to wash the dishes on a particular day of the week. One Thursday night it was Jennifer's turn to wash the dishes. She had a volleyball game at 7:00 p.m. and it was important that she not be late. She wanted to have her dishes washed before she went to the game, but most family members were still eating. Seeing her predicament, Jill said, "Jen, if you don't want to be late to your game, I'll do your dishes tonight if you'll do mine tomorrow." Jennifer was delighted; and as she ran out the door she said, "Thank you, thank you, Jill; that is so celestial of you." After the door closed, we ate in silence for a couple of minutes and then Jill said, "No, that wasn't really celestial of me. If I were celestial, I would offer to do her dishes tonight without making her do mine tomorrow." As I thought about Jill's comment, I realized she was right and I was surprised at the insight of an eleven-year-old.

Our family found that these ideas were very powerful; they made a great difference within our home. Simply striving to act more celestially created a much happier family atmosphere even though most of us seldom achieved the level to which we aspired.

## Beatitudes for Unhappy Families

The following beatitudes describe some of the common behaviors found in many families. Unfortunately, these beatitudes do not create happy families or lives of integrity. If parents want to create happy homes and rear responsible children, they need to do better than these beatitudes suggest.

1. *Blessed are they who tell the truth 99 percent of the time, for they shall be known as "basically" honest people.*

All of us describe ourselves as "basically" honest people even if we know we are occasionally dishonest. For the most part, we are content being "basically honest." But, people who are honest 99 percent of the time cannot be trusted. How could you ever trust me even if I only lied once in a hundred times? The answer is you can't, since you never know when that one time will be.

2. *Blessed are the deceitful, for they shall avoid disappointing others.*

The reason most children lie is to stay out of trouble. Children know their parents will be angry when they act irresponsibly, such as coming home late, damaging something valuable, or failing to do an assignment. Lying is often just a short-term solution to postpone the disappointment. Sometimes they don't intend to lie, they just need more time. They rationalize that damaged items can be fixed, lost items can be found, and chores can be done; so they are not really lying—they are just buying time.

When children lie to avoid disappointing parents, the reactions of both the parents and children should be considered. Perhaps the parents are not as understanding as they need to be. If parents have a habit of reacting harshly or extremely to small mistakes, it is easy to understand why children lie. Children are more willing to admit mistakes when their parents' reactions are reasonable and measured.

Children also need to realize that most parents will tolerate irresponsibility much better than they will tolerate dishonesty. It is easier to understand why a child failed to do a task than to accept lying about it. Parents need to teach the importance of honesty and dependability without overreacting to their children's failures.

3. *Blessed are they who use sarcasm, for they shall be known as funny and humorous people.*

Sarcasm is usually intended as a form of humor. Sarcastic comments are caustic and cutting comments that ridicule and taunt another person. Physical features, personal mannerisms, speech patterns, and unusual behaviors are often the focus of sarcastic comments. People often justify their sarcasm by claiming that it is funny, it makes people laugh, and it creates a happier group atmosphere. It is also excused by people who claim they would never say anything sarcastic unless they knew the other person understood they were just joking.

Although sarcasm may be funny, it is usually harmful to individuals and groups even when everyone knows it is only said in jest. People feel hurt by sarcastic comments and the group atmosphere becomes less secure and friendly even though people laugh. People know that if sarcasm is tolerated when it is directed toward others it will also be tolerated when it is directed against them.

4. *Blessed are the critical, for they shall look good in the eyes of others. Yea, confess thy spouse's sins.*

In an average day, most of us make numerous evaluative comments about the behaviors of others. Why do we do it? Sometimes people ask for feedback because they want it. When it is requested, we should try to provide feedback that is accurate but tactful. Comments that focus excessively on mistakes and inadequacies can be cruel and unkind; while comments that only describe the positive aspects may deprive the person of helpful feedback.

Most of our evaluations, however, are not requested and should never be said. We volunteer them for a variety of mostly selfish reasons. Sometimes we tell people what they did wrong because we think it will help them do better. For some reason, we are especially prone to criticize our spouse. Before doing so, however, we ought to assess whether our comments are really welcome and helpful. Usually they aren't.

Most of our criticisms are told to third parties and what we say should never be said. There is no good reason for such criticism. We only say it to feel powerful or look good. We describe the failings of others because it makes us appear knowledgeable and discerning. We should never say anything about people when they are absent that we would be embarrassed to say if they were present.

5. *Blessed are the selfish for they shall have the most toys at the end.*

Material possessions can be a great blessing when they are things we need. Some material possessions are necessary and they contribute enormously to our comfort and satisfaction. Consequently, our desire to acquire material possessions is based on a legitimate motive.

Unfortunately, the desire to acquire often turns into a hoarding instinct and we continue to amass resources that we can't use and don't need. Material possessions often serve as status symbols and we depend on our possessions to feel powerful and influential. Most of us have clothes, tools, toys, books, kitchen utensils, gardening equipment, camping gear, and many other household items that we will never use again. And these items could be a great blessing to others if we would give them away.

Family interactions are much more pleasant and supportive when members are willing to share freely with other members. Older children ought to ask themselves if there is any good reason why they shouldn't give clothing they have outgrown to their younger siblings. Some children refuse to share because they are afraid their things will get damaged. Others feel honored to have siblings use their things even if they get destroyed — indeed, they interpret the loss as an opportunity to sacrifice. This simple contrast in attitudes about sharing makes an enormous difference in family happiness.

6. *Blessed are they who shout the loudest, for they shall be heard.*

In our daily conversations, most of us are more interested in speaking than listening. When talking with another person we often want to dominate the "air time." If we don't think the other person is listening, we respond by speaking louder. When one person is speaking, the other should be listening. In most conversations, however, the listener concentrates less on what is being said than on what to say next. Instead of listening to what the other person is trying to say, we spend our time thinking about our next comment.

7. *Blessed are they who are right, for they shall win arguments.*

Most disagreements are interpreted as win-lose conflicts where one person wins and the other loses. We often overlook the possibility that both positions may be wrong. But even more distressing is the realization that when the disagreement is intense both sides lose regardless of the facts. Intense disagreements destroy interpersonal relationships and create bad feelings. No one wins an argument, regardless of who is technically *right*, if the disagreement destroys the interpersonal relationship between them. Happy family relationships are damaged by disagreements. In the end, it seldom matters which position was really right.

8. *Blessed are they who insist on getting their own way, for they shall obtain their independence.*

Getting our own way can be interpreted as evidence of our independence. When we have an idea in mind about how something should occur, most of us insist on having it done our way. We think our way is best and because we have taken time to think about it we feel justified in pressing our point. Getting our own way also makes us feel more in control and independent. If others disagree with us, they are free to go their own way and pursue their own course.

Unfortunately, this attitude of insisting on getting our own way is inconsistent with happy family relationships. Good relationships require sharing and joint planning. Family members need to recognize that greater satisfaction and joy comes from doing things together than by pursuing their individual interests. Independence is not the highest goal when it comes to creating happy families. The goal is not to be independent but to be interdependent.

9. *Blessed are they who swear for effect, for they shall influence others.*

Swearing basically represents the improper use of crude words to express feelings. It is viewed as evidence of an inadequate vocabulary and usually occurs when feelings are excessive and improper. When they are extremely upset, some parents think swearing is justified because it lets children know how they really feel. While it usually creates immediate attention, it fails to create the long-term effect parents actually want. Parents who teach children that swearing is wrong and an improper way to express their emotions cannot swear for effect without expecting to lose some of their children's respect and admiration.

10. *Blessed are they who are the biggest, for they can intimidate others with their size. After all, might makes right.*

Parents can influence children because they are bigger and stronger. When children are small, this size differential is helpful because children are not capable of responding to rational authority. But as children get bigger, parents need to develop better leadership skills to influence their children. Many teenagers are bigger and stronger than their parents and parents who have relied on physical strength to establish their superiority are in a difficult position.

The authority of parents to influence children does not depend on size or age. It stems from the obligation parents have to teach, provide for, and care for their children. As leaders in the home, parents need to remember the revealed advice regarding the proper use of authority: "No power or influence can or ought to be maintained by virtue of the priesthood, only by persuasion, by long-suffering, by gentleness and meekness, and by love unfeigned; By kindness, and pure knowledge, which shall greatly enlarge the soul without hypocrisy, and without guile."[16] Neither parents nor older siblings should use their size to intimidate or control the actions of younger children.

11. *Blessed are they who insist on listening to their own music and who play it loudly, for soon others will begin to love the same music.*

An appreciation for most cultural arts is acquired through a combination of experience and association. People have their own preferences for music, dance, drama, speech, and athletics. It makes just about as much sense to insist that a person like a particular work of art or music as for someone to insist that red is prettier than blue.

People, including teenagers, can acquire a love for the various cultural arts if they are willing to learn about them and experience them. But, forcing it on them usually has the opposite effect. Music is especially beautiful when it evokes beautiful memories; and a loud rock song can sound really great to someone who fell in love dancing to that song. All family members need to have patience when it comes to allowing others to enjoy their cultural interests. Someone who has a genuine love and concern for another person is likely to eventually acquire similar cultural preferences.

## What Kind Of Home Do You Want?

If parents want to have a celestial home, they need to behave celestially. They need to examine their own lives and assess how well they are treating others. Is your behavior telestial, terrestrial, or celestial?

What are your *motives*? Are you self-centered and focused on pursuing your own personal pleasures (telestial)? Do you focus on what is equal and fair (terrestrial)? Or do you focus on what you can do to serve and bless the lives of other family members (celestial)?

What are your *conversation* patterns? Do you gossip, criticize, swear, and make sarcastic comments (telestial)? Are your comments factual, accurate, and descriptive (terrestrial)? Or are they supportive, positive, expressive, and loving (celestial)?

What kind of *interactions* do you have with others? Do you try to see what you can get out of an exchange and negotiate in bad faith (telestial)? Do you follow the norm of reciprocity and insist on an equal exchange (terrestrial)? Or are you giving and sharing and primarily concerned about the welfare of the other (celestial)?

How do you exercise *authority* and how effectively do you lead? Are you demanding and autocratic for your own self-aggrandizement (telestial)? Do you establish rules and enforce them in a way that is fair and equal (terrestrial)? Or do you lead by example and see your leadership as an opportunity to serve and help those you lead (celestial)?

What kind of *social influence* do you exert on others? Are you power-oriented, controlling, and manipulative with a focus on who has the greatest influence on whom (telestial)? Do you focus on following rules and customs determined by a ruling coalition or majority opinion (terrestrial)? Or do you try to influence by example and encouragement with patience, kindness, and a genuine desire to build and nurture others (celestial)?

Even if only one family member decides to begin acting more celestially, the quality of family life will be substantially changed. In time others will observe and follow this member's example. When people first learn about telestial, terrestrial, and celestial behavior and consider behaving more celestially, their greatest concern is being abused: "I'll end up doing all the dishes." "If I didn't yell at them to clean the house and just did it myself, I'd spend the rest of my life picking up after them." "When my friends zing me I have to zing them back or I'll be treated like dirt all the time." Behaving celestially doesn't require you to do all the work or be abused. Most people find that even when they do more than their share, life is better and they are happier.

Some parents were raised in stable, loving homes by parents who were kind and faithful to each other. These parents have a distinct advantage when it comes to creating their own happy families. Children who come from stable homes have a good chance of creating their own healthy families. Children learn from their parents how to be good parents.

Unfortunately, an increasing number of children are being reared in homes where there is anger, infidelity, and violence. Dysfunctional families tend to produce dysfunctional children who usually create dysfunctional families of their own. But this cycle does not have to continue. People who come from homes filled with anger, abuse, and neglect can decide to stop the cycle now and not pass it on to the next generation.

At each given moment, we are free to choose how we will react to the situations we face. Perhaps our greatest human freedom is the freedom to decide how we will respond to an event. For example, if someone makes a rude comment to us, we can make a rude reply. But we are also free to ignore the comment or reply cheerfully. This freedom of choice is central to all human behavior.

If we have a habit of being rude when someone treats us unkindly, it may be difficult to break this habit. We may struggle not knowing how to react kindly. But *IF* we want to, we can try to be kind, and this is a personal choice we make for ourselves. Both parents and children can decide to do better. We each have the freedom to decide how we will react. Over time we develop habits that become well-ingrained personality traits. But regardless of how we have chosen to act in the past, at any given moment we can voluntarily decide to act differently.

## Summary

*Happy and healthy families don't just happen; they depend on following correct principles taught by the Savior.*

*Telestial people are self-centered and only concerned about their own selfish interests and lustful desires. Telestial behaviors create unhealthy, unhappy, and dysfunctional homes.*

*Terrestrial people are willing to make laws and abide by them. They are good people who accept the norm of reciprocity. Terrestrial behavior focuses on what is fair and just and what makes an equal exchange. Terrestrial behavior can create a stable, peaceful home; but, it does not provide an adequate moral foundation for rearing responsible children.*

*Celestial people are those who follow the pattern of living taught by Jesus Christ in the Sermon on the Mount. Celestial behaviors involve turning the other cheek, going the second mile, and loving one's enemy. These kinds of unselfish behaviors build happy and healthy homes and help children learn responsibility.*

# 3

# Effective
# Child-Rearing Practices

One of the most interesting lectures I have heard on child-rearing practices was delivered by a mother living in upstate New York. I was a twenty-year-old missionary for The Church of Jesus Christ of Latter-day Saints, and my companion and I met this woman as we were going door-to-door through a neighborhood. As we visited in the living room I observed a child in the kitchen struggling to make a peanut butter and honey sandwich. Three slices of bread were on the floor, along with the jar of peanut butter and the jar of honey. The child struggled for a long time trying to get the lid off the peanut butter jar. He was about three years old and his little hands could not hold the jar and twist the lid at the same time. Finally, in frustration, he brought the jar to his mother, who removed the lid.

A few minutes later I watched as the child spread globs of peanut butter on both the bread and the floor. At that point I volunteered to help the child fix a sandwich. In the back of my mind I think I was hoping the mother would invite me to fix myself one also. Instead, she very gently said, "No, he needs to do this by himself." I was content to have my services ignored until a few minutes later, when the child began to pour the honey on the bread. When the child started, the honey jar contained about two pounds of honey, but a few moments later almost half of it was on the floor.

I thought the child obviously needed help at this point, and since the mother was sitting with her back to the kitchen, I thought she would appreciate knowing what was happening. I tried to tactfully suggest that the child needed some help, but the mother didn't respond. By this point the child had both stepped and sat in the pool of honey, and I could only imagine what would happen as the child continued to move about the kitchen. If the mother would only look at the problem, I thought, she would realize the child needed help. In desperation I finally pointed at the floor and asked, "Isn't that a pool of honey on the floor?"

Finally, the mother turned around and observed what was happening. I was surprised by her calm response. Rather than moving immediately to contain the mess, she looked back at me and said, "Yes, that's honey on the floor."

"I think he sat in it, and it's going to get all over the kitchen," I said.

"It can be wiped up," she responded.

"But if he comes in here, won't it be difficult to wash the honey out of the carpet and furniture?" I asked.

She only replied, "It will be more difficult."

At that point, the mother began to explain her child-rearing philosophy. She said her goal was to raise children who would be independent and creative, who could think and act for themselves and live their lives free of arbitrary constraints of adults. If parents want children who are creative, independent, and think for themselves, she explained, then they must allow their children to make their own decisions at an early stage in life and begin doing things for themselves. Even before her children had reached their first birthday, she went on, she had involved them in deciding what they would eat and what they would wear. She believed that making children choose which breakfast cereal they wanted forced them to be independent and think for themselves.

After listening to this mother explain the benefits of a permissive, lenient approach to child rearing, I had to admit that it sounded very persuasive, but I still had a problem with the pool of honey on the floor. I wondered if there wasn't something better the mother could have done to handle the mess on the floor without destroying her child's freedom, creativity, and independent thinking. At that time the modern advice to parents supported this mother's lenient and permissive approach to child rearing. Subsequent research, however, has shown that these child-rearing practices fail to achieve the desired results.

## Child-Rearing Myths

The values and behaviors of children are significantly influenced by the way their parents treat them. Extensive research has examined the influence of various child-rearing practices and shown that lenient permissiveness is not the best practice. Instead, child-rearing practices that emphasize firm discipline, obedience to authority, close supervision, involvement with the child, and warm emotional support all contribute to the development of socially accepted values and personal responsibility in children.

These conclusions raise two rather disturbing concerns. The first concern is that close supervision and strict demands will create resistance and antagonism in children. Some parents fear that firmly enforcing rules in the home will cause their children to become hostile. Rebelliousness and running away from home have frequently been attributed to excessive parental control. "If we try to enforce too many rules, won't she rebel and run away from home?"

The second concern is that strict discipline and rule enforcement will create overly submissive children who will suffer a loss of individuality and self-assertiveness. Too much parental authority is sometimes believed to cause blind obedience. "If we always tell him exactly what to do, won't he come to depend on us all the time?" Blind obedience to rules and unquestioned compliance have been attributed to the way parents exercise arbitrary authority and teach children to obey. Consequently, strict discipline has been condemned because of the horrible atrocities committed by people who blindly obeyed authority, such as the My Lai massacre, the mass killings in the German prison camps, the Jonestown suicides, and the ethnic cleansing in Bosnia. Some have suggested that children should be subjected to only limited amounts of parental authority or none at all.

These popular ideas about the evils of strict discipline and the desirability of permissive parenting are not supported by numerous studies on the effects of child-rearing practices. The research indicates that firm discipline does not necessarily create either aggressive antagonism or submissive compliance. On the contrary, firm discipline has been shown to contribute to socially responsible and independent behavior in children.

Several significant contributions have been made in recent times to our understanding of effective child-rearing practices. The literature reviews and research of Diana Baumrind, a member of the Psychology Department of the University of California at Berkeley, have been especially useful in explaining the effects of parental control, obedience to authority, and discipline on children's moral and social development.[17] Baumrind reviewed the results of twelve studies on child-rearing practices and concluded that the evidence did not support some of the popular ideas about child discipline.

One of the major myths these studies failed to support was that rebelliousness in children, particularly adolescents, is caused by close parental supervision, high demands, and other manifestations of parental authority. On the contrary, the studies found that higher demands were made by the parents of children who were the least hostile or delinquent. Firm parental control was associated with responsible conscience development in children. Baumrind suggested that affection and concern needed to accompany those high parental demands. Parents who demanded that their children be orderly and assume household responsibilities also seemed to provide surroundings that contributed to the children's well-being, and they tended to involve themselves conscientiously in their children's welfare. Perhaps the parents' strict demands were viewed by the children as reasonable and did not provoke rebellion because the children believed their parents had a genuine concern for their welfare. Additional studies have indicated that parental demands provoke rebellion only when the parents are also repressive, hostile, and restrictive.

A second myth was also not supported by the studies. This myth suggested that firm parental control generates passivity and dependence. Generally, the most self-reliant children came from parents who demanded obedience and were rated highest in firm control.

A similar myth, that parental restrictiveness decreases self-assertiveness and buoyancy, was also not supported. Delinquent boys, for example, tended to come from non-restrictive homes where parents made very few demands of their children and were not highly controlling. Nondelinquent boys, however, came from more restrictive homes in which parents created explicit expectations for behavior, exerted firm discipline, and required rule compliance. The studies indicated that parental restrictiveness decreases self-assertiveness only when it is accompanied by hostility and overprotectiveness.

Another myth Baumrind examined was that permissiveness frees the child from the authority of the parent. Permissiveness not only failed to generate individualism and self-reliant behavior, it also increased the incidence of aggression. When parents did not discipline the child for aggressive behavior, their failure to respond was interpreted by the child as accepting aggressiveness.

These findings suggest that parental control and discipline do not produce the negative effects that many have feared. Instead, parental control, discipline, and obedience to authority are essential for children to develop moral responsibility. Simplistic ideas, such as "permissiveness produces individuality," fail to consider the significant role that discipline and obedience to a rational authority play in the developmental process.

## Authoritative Parents

Besides dispelling some of the popular myths about the effects of parental discipline and control, Diana Baumrind provided an alternative model of parental influence.  In addition to the typical dichotomy of *permissive* versus *authoritarian* control, she described a third model, called *authoritative* control, and provided evidence to show that it creates well-socialized behavior as well as willful and independent behavior in children.

*Permissive* parents, according to Baumrind, are non-punitive, acceptant, and affirmative toward their children's impulses, desires, and actions.  They consult with their children about policy decisions and family rules and make very few demands on them for household responsibility and orderly behavior. Permissive parents present themselves to their children as resources for them to use as they wish, not as ideals for them to emulate or as active agents responsible for shaping or altering their behavior.  They allow and encourage their children to regulate their activities as much as possible and avoid exercising control or encouraging them to obey externally defined standards.  To obtain compliance from their children when necessary, they attempt to use reason and manipulation but not overt power.  The mother at the beginning of this chapter advocated a permissive child-rearing philosophy that permitted children to be self-regulated, free of restraints, and unconcerned about the expression of impulse or the effects of their carelessness.

*Authoritarian* parents, unlike permissive parents, attempt to shape, control, and evaluate the behavior and attitudes of their children according to a set standard of conduct, usually an absolute standard that is based upon a higher authority. Authoritarian parents value obedience as a virtue and favor punitive, forceful measures to control their children when their children's actions or beliefs conflict with what they think is proper. They believe in keeping their children in place, in restricting their independence, and in assigning household responsibilities in order to teach respect for work. They regard the preservation of order and traditional structures as a highly valued end in itself. They do not encourage a verbal give-and-take with their children, believing that children should accept their word without question.

Authoritarian parents are not necessarily harsh and stern. While they are strict and consistent, they can also be loving and concerned. However, their authority is complete and they assume no obligation to justify their rules, explain their directives, or discuss alternatives with their children.

*Authoritative* parents attempt to direct their children's activities in a rational, issue-oriented manner. They encourage verbal give-and-take, and share with their children the reasoning behind their policies, and solicit their objections when they attempt to resist. Both independent self-will and disciplined conformity are valued by authoritative parents. Therefore, they exert firm control at points of parent-child divergence, but they do not hem in the child with restrictions. They enforce their own perspectives as adults, but they recognize their children's individual interests and special ways. Authoritative parents affirm the child's present qualities, but also set standards for future conduct. They use reason, power, and shaping by reinforcement to achieve their objectives, and do not base their decisions on group consensus or on their children's desires.

The behavioral differences between authoritative and authoritarian parents seem rather small, but they produce a significant difference in the behavior of children. Both kinds of parents take an active role in shaping the child's behavior. Both exercise power to obtain obedience, exert firm discipline and rule enforcement, and disapprove of their children's defiance. But they differ in the extent to which they encourage independence and individuality. Unlike authoritarian parents, authoritative parents define the child's individuality clearly, encourage intimate verbal contact, display empathetic understanding, and give reasons for their directives.

In a series of studies, Baumrind and her associates observed children at school while assessing their parents through structured interviews and home visits. The results indicated that the children of authoritative parents were the most socially responsible, self-reliant, self-controlled, explorative, and content. The children of authoritarian parents were also socially responsible; but they were somewhat discontent, withdrawn, and distrustful, and they also lacked independence. Permissive parents were non-controlling, non-demanding, and relatively warm, but they did not produce independent children. The children of permissive parents were the least self-reliant, the least explorative, and the least self-controlled. Furthermore, the children of permissive parents were generally lacking in social responsibility.

To explain why authoritative parental control produced well-socialized and independent children, Baumrind reexamined the concept of freedom. She rejected the idea that freedom means giving children the liberty to do as they please without interference from adult guardians. Instead, she defined freedom as the *appreciation of necessity*. That is, children gain freedom by understanding the nature of the outside world and controlling their reactions to it. This concept of freedom implies the power to act rather than the absence of external control.

The implications of this definition are profound. It suggests that independence and individuality develop not by the absence of controls but by the presence of appropriate controls that help children master their environment.

## Discipline and Obedience.

Another fascinating study focusing on a much different problem, the problem of drug abuse among teenagers, also supports the value of discipline and parental control. Richard H. Blum and his associates, who worked mostly for the Institute of Public Policy

Analysis at Stanford University, wanted to discover why some children succumbed to environmental pressures and began using illicit drugs while other children successfully resisted these social pressures. Their research showed that family influences were the important factors governing the use of illicit drugs. Thus, their study is really a study of family interactions and parental child-rearing practices.[18]

The study covered blue-collar white families, blue-collar black families, Mexican-American families, and "hippie" families. However, the largest and most extensively studied group consisted of 101 white middle-class families. These families all lived in the same area. Both mother and father lived at home and they had at least one child at college and younger children in the home. In many respects, the researchers said, all 101 families could be considered solid, respectable, middle-class American families.

Each family was classified as a high-, medium-, or low-risk family according to the drug use of the children. The risk score was based on both the frequency of use and kind of drugs used, and referred to both the present and the potential danger. Thus, high-risk families had one or more children who frequently used opiates, cocaine, LSD, or other illicit drugs. There was no illicit drug use in low-risk families.

Several major differences were found between the high- and low-risk families. Low-risk families were more likely to be politically conservative and to attend church regularly. High-risk families tended to reject all major political parties and did not attend church. Low-risk families were father-led or authoritative families in which the father supervised schoolwork and had the last word on health practices, major purchases, and the like. There was less freedom of choice for younger children in low-risk families, but older children seemed to go about their activities without fuss as though choices were their own. In high-risk families, the concept of discipline was not emphasized as a required part of child-rearing. Children were given greater freedom of choice at an earlier age on everything except their study habits.

The parents were given a list of ten child-rearing goals and asked to rank their importance. Low-risk parents emphasized teaching the child self-control, whereas high-risk parents emphasized expanding the child's creative potential and preparing the child for a world of change.

The children mirrored their parents' attitudes and values. When asked to rank a list of ten child-rearing goals, low-risk children gave high priority to turning the child into a respectable citizen, teaching self-control, and teaching obedience. High-risk children gave high priority to helping the child become a loving person and to expanding the child's creative capacity. When asked at what age they should be allowed to decide things for themselves, high-risk children set earlier ages than low-risk children for deciding about friends, bedtimes, church attendance, belief in God, how much liquor to drink, political activities, hairstyles, where to go for fun, whom to date, sexual intercourse, use of marijuana, and when to respect the police.

Differences were also reported in the work experiences of high- and low-risk families. Low-risk children began participating in family chores earlier than high-risk children. More than half of the low-risk families encouraged the child to begin chores before the age of six, whereas high-risk families frequently waited until the child was nine years old. Yard work in particular was more often assigned to children in low-risk families.

To some people the lifestyle of the low-risk families appears to combine the worst aspects of a military dictatorship and prison life. Some might argue that the fathers of low-risk families are much like drill instructors in the military. Nevertheless, low-risk families successfully immunized their children against the use of drugs even though drugs abounded in their neighborhoods and schools. But did these families use such strict discipline that it produced mindless submissiveness or a loss of individuality? Does the authoritative discipline of the low-risk family have any value in addition to reducing drug abuse?

The final project undertaken by Blum and his associates was an intensive clinical investigation of thirteen families who had been interviewed earlier. These families were observed by a researcher who visited them in their homes as a dinner guest. The families also participated in videotaped group discussions with a narcotics officer, a minister, and a girl with "hippie-like appearance and attitudes." The topic of the discussion centered on what children should be taught about drugs. Two psychoanalytically trained professionals also observed the families and made independent evaluations of the quality of family interaction. The goal was to learn whether the drug risk score determined earlier corresponded to the clinicians' ratings of the excellence of family interactions.

In general, the families' drug risk scores were closely associated with the ratings of family interactions. For example, none of the families rated superior or good came from the high-risk group, whereas the families rated as troubled or pathological in their interactions were all high-risk families. Low-risk families tended to produce a climate that was conducive to the emotional growth of their children. The family circle was generally happy and family members enjoyed being together.

Perhaps the most profound paradox of Blum's study was the inability of high-risk children to participate in the group discussions. High-risk parents had indicated that they wanted their children to be creative and independent, yet high-risk children were generally incapable of participating openly in the group discussions. High-risk children were the least creative and the least able to think for themselves. They seemed to be easily influenced by the arguments of others and complained most about restrictions of their freedom.

The low-risk children participated most aggressively in the group discussions. They argued for their point of view and tried to persuade the "hippie" girl to their "straight" way of thinking. Low-risk parents had placed high values on discipline, self-control, respect for the rights of others, and obedience to God's commands. Once their children had internalized these values, they were free to develop their own individuality. They had learned the rules of the game and had demonstrated to their parents that they had sufficient discipline and self-control to direct their own behavior. Their parents trusted them and approved of the decisions they made.

The studies of Baumrind and Blum and their associates demonstrate the significance of obedience and discipline within the home. These results indicate that personal responsibility and socially desirable values are primarily developed through a process of child-rearing that involves strong family expectations for good performance, work experiences in early childhood, religious commitments, and individual initiative.

Other studies have supported these same findings. A study in 1948, for example, found that effective work adjustment was associated with family backgrounds characterized by a closely knit family group in which children have early work experiences and where religious values and church attendance are stressed. Four other studies found, as did Blum, that the avoidance of drugs and alcohol is related to similar family characteristics.[19]

## Summary

*Strict discipline and close parental supervision do not cause children to become rebellious or overly submissive.*

*Permissive and lenient child-rearing practices do not help children become creative, independent, or socially responsible. Permissiveness does not free children from parental authority.*

*Authoritative parents who have strict expectations, exert firm discipline, and are willing to explain their demands tend to raise socially responsible and well-adjusted children.*

*Child-rearing practices that emphasize firm discipline, obedience to authority, close supervision, involvement with the child, and warm emotional support all contribute to the development of socially-accepted values and personal responsibility in children. Also important are practices that emphasize strong family expectations for good performance, work experiences in early childhood, religious commitments, and individual initiative.*

# 4

# Developing
# Responsibility

At a summer youth camp, all of the youth were expected to participate in the camp chores program. The jobs were posted on the camp bulletin board, and the youth were expected to assign themselves to a daily job, such as preparing and serving food, washing dishes, or cleaning and repairing the camp. Each task required about one hour, and the incentive for performing the task was a token that could only be used in a vending machine that dispensed ice cream bars. Although the work was semi-supervised by adults, no one supervised the sign-up. The youth were simply told that they were expected to perform one task per day and were encouraged to select a variety of tasks.

After the second day at camp the vending machine was rigged so that an ice cream bar could be removed without inserting a token. Before long the secret of the faulty vending machine was rumored throughout the camp. The young people were still expected to participate in the daily work assignments, and they still received tokens. But no longer did they need a token to get an ice cream bar. By the end of the week, many of the job assignments were not being filled, and the number of tokens inserted into the vending machine was far less than the number of ice cream bars that were removed. The integrity of the young people was challenged further by a note from the camp director acknowledging that the vending machine was temporarily broken and asking that they put their tokens in the slot anyway.

The broken vending machine provided an interesting opportunity to examine the values of the youth. Which young people would continue working for a token that was no longer needed? Which ones would leave their tokens in the machine when they took their ice cream bar?

On one occasion three fourteen-year-old boys came to the vending machine to get their ice cream bars. The first boy discovered he could get his ice cream bar without inserting his token, whereupon the second boy withdrew two ice cream bars without inserting a token—one for himself and one for the third fellow. The third boy thanked him for the ice cream bar but inserted his token into the vending machine.

Before the week ended, this occurred three times. Each time one fellow insisted on paying for his ice cream bar even though his friends told him they thought it was silly to pay for something they could get for free. Before he went home this fellow was asked why he insisted on paying for his ice cream bars. His answer was simply, "My parents always taught me to be helpful and to pay my own way. It would have been dishonest for me to keep the token." When the other fellows were asked, they admitted that taking the ice cream bars without leaving a token was wrong and they knew so at the time. But they thought it was "no big deal."

This story illustrates two basic components of teaching values. The first component consists of establishing standards of appropriate behavior— knowing what is right and wrong. The second component consists of internalizing those standards. Children first need to know what is acceptable behavior; for example, they are expected to earn the tokens and exchange them for an ice cream bar. Second, they need to feel an internal obligation to do what they are expected to do. Knowing what is right does not mean they will always choose the right. The value of honesty has to be internalized as a basic element in their value system if they are to always act with integrity.

Two processes contributing to value internalization are *induction* and *modeling*. Induction refers to the teaching process—presenting new ideas, explaining new concepts, and sharing new information. Modeling refers to the example set by others. Individuals observe the behavior of others and then follow or model their behavior. Parents should teach and model celestial behavior.

## Induction:  The Teaching Process

The greatest lessons for parents to teach in their day-to-day child-rearing are the teachings of the Savior. These simple teachings, described in chapter 2, explain the celestial behaviors that both children and adults should try to follow. These insights provide an eternal perspective for teaching social values and they provide a moral foundation to guide our daily actions.

In their daily interactions with children, parents need to explain the reasons for their expectations. Why is it wrong to steal? Why should I practice the piano? Why is it wrong to hit someone who is mean to me? Why should I do this dumb job?

The benefit of a patient explanation is particularly obvious when parents ask children to perform a task; children need to know the purpose of the job. Work without a purpose is drudgery. But when there is a purpose, even some of the most unpleasant jobs become tolerable. Parents need to be particularly sympathetic to the short attention span of young children who may have a difficult time understanding why a clean playroom makes the house look better or helps to prevent toys from being broken. Providing a rationale for the task contributes to the child's motivation to perform it. If you have carefully decided why you want a job done, you should not have difficulty presenting a reasonable rationale for it.

Many parents expect their children to obey them simply because they are the parents. This is not only an abuse of parental power but a poor way to teach responsibility. Children deserve at least some explanation if they are old enough to understand. If you explain the reason why a job is important, the child will feel a greater motivation to perform it.

An adequate explanation for some actions is that they are commandments of God, period. Fornication, masturbation, lying, profanity, and stealing are sinful because God has condemned them. Rational explanations of the long-term consequences of sinful behavior might help motivate children to obey; but, they are expected to obey even if they don't understand the long-term consequences. The commandments of God are explained in the scriptures, and parents who know and use the scriptures can help their children understand why they should live a moral life. When children want to know why God says something is wrong, explain it as well as you can. But you are not required to provide an eloquent, logical justification, and you should not be reluctant to say, in effect, "I know not, save the Lord has commanded it."

Parents should have no difficulty explaining the justifications for the jobs they assign if they have thought about them sufficiently. There are a lot of good reasons why children should pick up their toys, clean their rooms, study their homework, wash the dishes, practice the piano, and help with the yard work. When there isn't time to explain, an adequate reason should be, "Because it needs to be done, and I said to do it." However, as a general rule parents should avoid exercising arbitrary power; you should have rational reasons for your requests, and you should be willing to explain them.

In addition to explaining the *specific purpose* of a task, parents need to provide a general explanation for the purpose of work. Here, the explanation goes beyond the purpose of the specific task, and explains the meaning of work. Work is defined as an activity that produces useful products or services to your family or society. Children need to see work as a useful activity beyond the benefit of the specific task being considered.

To help children acquire a general value for work, parents use a variety of proverbs and adages. A general principle that has served well as a rule of conduct is, "If it's worth doing, it's worth doing right." Over the years this proverb has been used by countless mothers as they have attempted to encourage their children to take pride in their work. (The modern version of this proverb is, "If it's worth doing, it's worth doing for money.") The following is a list of other frequently heard proverbs or family mottos that parents have taped on mirrors, attached to refrigerators, used as bookmarks, and repeated while working with children:

"A place for everything and everything in its place."
"Plan your work and then work your plan."
"Happiness isn't doing what you like to do but  liking what you have to do."
"Hard work will get you anywhere you want to go in the world."
"There is no end to the amount of good you can accomplish in this life if you don't worry about who gets the credit."
"Cleanliness is next to godliness."
"If you do it right the first time, you won't have to come back and do it a second time."
"Don't ask the Lord to guide your footsteps unless you're willing to move your feet."
"Pray for a crop, but keep hoeing."

The importance of providing a rationale for your expectations was demonstrated by the research described in chapter 3. The major difference between authoritative and authoritarian parents was the willingness of authoritative parents to provide a reasonable explanation for their demands. Strict obedience and firm parental expectations are characteristic of both authoritarian and authoritative parents. The authoritarian parent, however, issues commands and demands compliance without explaining the reasons for these demands, while an authoritative parent assumes the responsibility of helping the child understand why the commands are important.

## Modeling: The Example of Parents

Parents err if they think they only teach values by the things they say. Obviously, what they say is important. But if what they say is inconsistent with what they do, their behavior will usually speak louder than their words. In fact, the example of parents is often the most profound teacher of personal values.

When children follow the example of parents, this process is called "modeling." Children model or pattern their behavior after the behavior of their parents. This process is also referred to as "imitative behavior" because children first learn how to behave by imitating their parents. Illustrations of imitative behavior can be observed in almost everything children do—the way they smile, the way they talk, the slang they use, the way they comb their hair, table manners, food preferences, the way they sit, the way they express appreciation, and they way they pray. Although parents may be too close to their children to observe the pervasive influence of their own modeling, they usually notice it in other families.

Imitative behavior is particularly strong when the model is an attractive, high-status person. Research studies have shown, for example, that fathers tend to exert a stronger influence on their children's behavior when they are perceived as attractive and well liked than when they are disliked or of lower status. Research studies have also shown that modeling is particularly effective when the situation is uncertain and ambiguous. Because children face so many uncertain and ambiguous situations, the examples of their parents are very important.

So what do parents do when their behavior is not consistent with the values they want to teach? Can parents effectively teach children to do something they do not do themselves? Can a mother teach a daughter to keep her room clean when the rest of the house looks like a tornado has struck? The answer depends largely on the sincerity of the parents' motives. Mothers will not be very successful in teaching their daughters to be neat and tidy unless they exemplify these traits. The example of parents is a very powerful teacher, and it is difficult for parents to say anything that is more impressive than the impact of what they do.

For several years a couple thought their daughter would be raised as an only child, but then things changed. In a period of four years, three more children were added to the family. Keeping the house clean was not too difficult when there were only three people, but three additional children created continual spills, messes, and a lot of dirty diapers. The oldest daughter, Stacey, was thirteen when the fourth child was born, and she resented having to help with the housework. Until recently, Stacey had not been asked to help with the meals, clean the house, or even make her own bed. But now the mother had more pressing demands on her time than to pick up after Stacey and wait on her as she had done before. In addition to the constant demands of three small children, the mother also had to help her husband with his delivery business. Her job was to answer the phone, which rang constantly. Her husband provided almost no assistance with the housework, partly because he was seldom home and partly because he had a disability that restricted the use of one hand. The mother realized that the house was a mess, and realized also that it would get worse unless Stacey assisted with some of the housework.

As a minimum, the mother decided Stacey should be responsible for cleaning her own bedroom. There was no reason why Stacey couldn't make her own bed, clean her room, and take care of her clothes. The rest of the house might be a mess, but Stacey's room at least ought to be clean. The mother's concern was whether she could expect Stacey to clean her own room while she as the mother did such a poor job keeping the rest of the house clean.

Whether parents can teach their children to do something they do not do themselves is an issue that applies to many areas in the parent-child relationship. Can parents who do not attend church themselves teach their children the importance of church attendance? Can a father who has spent four years in prison for embezzling company funds teach his children to be honest? Can parents who started their family before they were married effectively teach their children the importance of chastity? Can parents who flunked out of school teach their children the importance of good study habits?

Hypocrisy means to pretend to be what you are not or to feel what you do not feel. The pretense of virtue was one of the major criticisms against society voiced by college students during the youth rebellion of the seventies. College students across the country accused college administrators, parents, and government officials of being hypocrites.

There is, however, an important difference between being hypocritical and sincerely attempting to teach proper values. The critical difference is in the sincerity of the parents' motives and behavior. If Stacey's mother had ample opportunity to keep the house clean and yet failed to do so, her expectations would be hypocritical and she would have very little success teaching Stacey to clean her own room. But because of the demands of helping with her husband's business and caring for three younger children, the mother should have no hesitancy in expecting Stacey to clean her own room. In fact, Stacey should be expected to do considerably more than just clean her own room. As a teenager, Stacey should be mature enough to recognize the demands of the situation and help extensively with the housework. Stacey should be taught how to clean the house, prepare meals, care for her younger brothers and sister, and even assist her father by taking telephone messages.

Likewise, fathers who have spent time in prison for embezzlement should be able to teach a very powerful lesson to their children about the evils of theft. Parents who have done poorly in school should be able to teach a very powerful lesson about the importance of good study habits. It is not unreasonable for parents to teach their children to be better than they were. Parents who have made mistakes should strive to help their children avoid making the same mistakes. Sincere parents can use their failures as excellent teaching illustrations to help their children. In doing so, however, it is necessary for the parents to acknowledge the fact that they made a mistake and to express genuine regret for having made it. Children are generally very tolerant and forgiving of their parents' mistakes. However, parents cannot continue to make the same mistakes and still convince their children that they expect them to do better. If the house is dirty because the mother spends countless hours watching soap operas during the day, the mother's demands that others clean their rooms will appear hypocritical. In shaping their children's values and behavior, parents should remember that it is not what they have done in the past that counts as much as what they are doing in the present, and what they are committed to do in the future.

## Value Internalization Process

The value internalization process consists of systematically acquiring general values that become part of a person's fundamental character. This process requires a considerable amount of thinking about what is morally right and proper, combined with a moral motivation to do what is right and fair because of internally-based justifications. The following story helps to illustrate some of the basic elements of the value internalization process.

"When I was a kid, I spent most of my summer vacations clipping a hedge along the side of our property. My mother used that strip of grass to teach me how to work. In my memory, the hedge was at least one hundred feet long, but when I took my children back to see it, I was surprised to discover that it was only about fifty feet. It consisted of a row of bushes with a five-foot incline covered with grass on the other side. My brother and I were responsible for the job, and mother convinced us that to do it right, the grass had to be clipped with a small pair of hand clippers. The incline was too steep and bumpy to use a push mower, and so every two weeks we found ourselves starting at the back of the hedge and working toward the front yard.

"If I had a power mower and some electric clippers today, I'm sure I could keep that hedge looking immaculate in less than thirty minutes per week. But with our little hand clippers and a lot of dawdling, clipping the hedge was a full-time summer job. Every time I wanted to go swimming or play with my friends, my mother's standard question was, 'Have you clipped the hedge yet?' The answer was always 'No' because the hedge was never done. The grass on that incline never stopped growing. Obviously mother realized that, and she was usually content to let us play after we had worked a couple of hours."

Value internalization involves a three-step process in which the individual's motive advances from (1) compliance to (2) identification to (3) internalization, and the individual's cognitive (or intellectual) development advances from (1) a belief about a specific act to (2) a belief in a general consequence to (3) a belief in principles of right and wrong. This process is illustrated in figure 1. The motive changes from the benefit that is acquired through a specific act, to the benefit that comes from a general consequence, to a belief in doing what is right simply because it is right.

At the first step of this process, individuals perform a specific act because it creates immediate benefits. The basic motive here is compliance in order to seek rewards and avoid punishment. For example, the person in the story above first clipped the hill only because his mother said he had to do it, not because he wanted to work or because he enjoyed clipping the hedge. In essence, he was saying to himself, "I will do this job as long as the immediate advantages outweigh the immediate disadvantages."

Through induction and modeling, the child's value orientation advances to the second level, in which value is ascribed to the general consequences of a range of behaviors rather than just a specific act. Instead of being specific to a single situation, the value now applies to a broad range of related behaviors. The basic motive at this level is identification; that is, we want to please others by acting like them or doing as they say. Here the child goes from a belief in the purpose of this specific job to a belief in the purpose of work in general. Clipping the hill and other yard work contribute to the beauty of the home, make the yard look better, or make someone else happier. In essence, the child says to himself,

| *Level 1* | *Level 2* | *Level 3* |
|---|---|---|
| Compliance: "I want to obtain rewards and avoid punishment." | Identification: "I want to please others." | Internalization: "I want to do what is right." |
| Specific Act (situationally specific) | General consequence (rule oriented) | Principles of Right and Wrong (based on principle) |
| A belief in the purpose of *this specific job:* | A belief in the purpose of work in general: | A belief in doing what is right because it is right: |
| "I clip the hill only because it makes the yard look better or because someone says I have to do it; not because I like to work or want to do it." | "Clipping the hill and other forms of work (as a general rule) contribute to the beauty of our home, make our yard look better, or make someone happy." | "Clipping the hill and making the yard look attractive are the right things to do." |
| "I will do it as long as the immediate advantages outweigh the immediate disadvantages." | "I will do it and other similar activities as long as they are needed; in other words, as long as the long-term consequences are greater than the long-term costs." | "I do it because it's right. Whether it is fun or whether there are other things to do that are more fun are not relevant considerations." |

**Figure 1: The Value Internalization Process**

"I'll do the work I'm told to do if it is important to someone else and contributes in a positive way."

As parents continue to teach their children the importance of doing the right thing and doing it well, the child's value orientation advances from a belief in the general purpose of work to a belief in doing what is right simply because it is right. Level three is a very mature level that only a few adolescents normally reach. At level three the basic motivation is *internalization*. The individual's behavior is motivated by principles of right and wrong. The focus is on the act itself rather than the consequences of the act. The consequences of the act are not necessarily ignored; instead, they are carefully considered to help the individual decide whether the act is right or wrong. The illustration above obviously assumes that the task is worth doing and that there are positive consequences for doing it; clipping the hedge makes the yard look better and contributes to the beauty of the yard. If the consequences were negative, the activity would be redefined as the wrong thing to do. Someone at the third level of value internalization would say to himself, "Clipping the hedge and making the yard look attractive are the right things to do. Therefore I will clip the hedge." Whether it is fun or whether other things would be more fun are not relevant considerations.

## The Teaching Moment

When is the best time for parents to explain a new idea or teach a new insight to their children? Parents are constantly teaching by example, but when is the best time for them to make a conscious attempt to explain a principle or to provide a rationale for the importance of doing things right? This issue was studied in one of the classic research experiments in the 1920s by Dr. Hugh Hartshorne and Dr. Mark May evaluating the development of honesty and character.[20] As part of a series of experiments, they wanted to assess the effectiveness of daily lessons on honesty. In this particular study, a group of children was divided into an experimental group and a control group equated for age, sex, and intelligence. At the beginning, honesty tests were administered to both groups to obtain a baseline level of individual integrity. Three weeks later the experimental group began receiving fifteen-minute daily lessons about the importance of honesty. The lessons consisted of interesting stories of honest and dishonest behavior and discussions of the problems of honesty as it appears in various life situations.

After the experimental group received honesty lessons for three weeks, the honesty of both groups was again measured. The effectiveness of the teaching was evaluated by comparing the changes between the pre-test and post-test honesty scores for both groups. The researchers expected  no change in the honesty scores of the control group while the experimental group was expected to show a significant increase in honesty scores. To their surprise, however, the scores did not increase; instead there was a decrease in honesty in both groups with the control group showing the greatest decrease. Hartshorne and May were at a loss to explain these results. Several confounding variables may have contributed to the results, such as a lack of accuracy in the honesty tests or other variables  that influenced the children. Regardless of the explanation, it appears safe to conclude that regular conscious attempts on the part of parents to teach values are not as effective as the teaching that occurs during a teaching moment. The best time to explain new insights and teach personal values is during a teaching moment.

• While the grandparents are visiting, the mother asks a child to assist in serving the dessert. As the pie is placed on the plate, however, the mother discovers that more than pie is on the unclean plate. This is an excellent opportunity for the mother to explain the importance of careful dishwashing.

• While his friends are waiting outside to go swimming, Jim can't find his swimming suit. He distinctly remembers bringing it home yesterday, but can't remember what he did with it. While Jim's mother is helping him find it, this is an excellent time for her to explain why Jim should take care of his personal belongings and avoid being careless.

- After watching a program on television in which a parent and a child had a serious disagreement, the parents can ask their own children what caused the disagreement and what both parties should have done differently.
- After an older sibling has been disciplined for disobedience, the parents can discuss the importance of obedience with younger children who have observed the encounter.

Parents need to realize that very little effective teaching occurs during the heat of anger. When tempers are high and emotions are strong neither parents nor children can be expected to think very rationally. Basketball players, for example, should not wait until their fifth foul is called on them near the end of the game to decide the appropriate way to respond to a bad call by a referee. Fifteen minutes before the Pinewood Derby when your son discovers that his sister has broken one of the wheels on the car is not the time to remind your son that he teases his sister too much.

It is difficult for anyone to behave very rationally or think very clearly when emotions are running hot. For example, the parents of a teenager knew their son had a hot temper and would get easily upset. When he became upset, he would start to grumble and complain until he became so angry he would turn and walk away. His parents were disturbed by his behavior, but for several months they decided to ignore it. They hoped he would learn to behave better when he saw how his friends were turned off by his anger. Unfortunately, the situation was not resolved as the parents had anticipated. They saw their son get angry at his friends and walk out on them. But rather than realizing the consequences of his behavior and learning to control his temper, the son persisted in making the same mistake. The parents soon discovered that instead of learning from his experience, their son was losing his friends. Finally the parents realized that they would have to find times when their son was calm, rational, and able to think objectively about his behavior to teach him the consequences of losing his temper and getting angry. When he was angry and upset, the parents found that their comments were grossly misunderstood, distorted, and perceived as threats and criticism. The parents finally learned to say, "Let's talk about this after you've cooled down." A few minutes delay made a world of difference. The time to decide how to behave is not during the heat of the battle, but during quiet times when we can think rationally and objectively— when we can calmly determine what is the best way to behave.

To teach values, parents need to take advantage of teaching moments. Working alongside your children creates unique opportunities to teach moral and personal values. These teaching moments can have an unusually strong impact on your child's personal values. At these times, most of the proverbs parents are prone to express have their greatest significance and impact on the life of the child. "If it's worth doing, it's worth doing right." "A place for everything, and everything in its place."

If parents are sensitive to a situation, they can find numerous teaching opportunities. However, you do not need to wait for a teaching moment to occur naturally; you can create one. The father of a high-school football star, for example, became increasingly concerned that football was becoming too important to his son and his success on the football field was making him extremely self-centered. One night when he knew his son did not have any scheduled activities, the father called his son from the office and told him he needed to have him accompany him that night on a special assignment. When the son asked what he would be doing the father simply said that it would take too long to explain, but that it was very important. When the father arrived at the home, he immediately picked up the son and headed for the local children's hospital. The father had told the hospital staff that he would be there with his son simply to visit some of the disabled youth. When they arrived at the hospital, the father introduced his son to a three-year-old girl and suggested that he tell her the story of "Goldilocks and the Three Bears" while he went next door to visit another child. He told many other stories before the evening ended. On their way home they stopped for hamburgers and had a chance to visit together. The father was pleased to learn that his son had promised the three-year-old girl he would return the following week to tell her another story.

## Summary

*Two components of teaching values are (a) establishing standards of appropriate behavior and (b) internalizing these standards.*

*The processes contributing to value internalization are induction and modeling, i.e., teaching by precept and example.*

*Internalizing values occurs in three steps: (a) believing in a specific act and doing what is right because of the immediate benefit (compliance), (b) believing in broadly defined activities and doing what is right because of the long-term consequences, usually to please others (identification), and (c) believing in general principles of behavior and accepting them because they are right (internalization).*

*The most effective time to teach moral values is during a teaching moment.*

# 5

# Characteristics of
# Outstanding Workers

"As the twig is bent, so grows the tree." This proverb should not make you feel anxious about minor confrontations with your children. You should not overreact to small things like poorly washed dishes or unmade beds, and assume these problems are serious indications of irresponsible behavior. Children make many mistakes, and you will feel frustrated and disappointed if your expectations are too high.

At the same time, however, you need to realize that the directions children pursue in their early childhood create a lasting impact on their later life. Responsible parenting creates responsible children, and responsible children become responsible adults.

## A Survey of Work Values

Adults' values are significantly influenced by their early childhood experiences. A study examining the work values of adult employees illustrated the tremendous influence of child-rearing practices on the development of personal responsibility. This study used questionnaires and interviews to survey the attitudes and values of over three thousand workers.[21] The questionnaire measured an assortment of background variables and attitudes toward specific jobs, toward the company, toward the community, and toward work in general.  When the responses were analyzed, five items associated with their family backgrounds were the best predictors of their work values.

1. "My family expects me to perform well on the job."
2. "How important is religion in your life?"
3. "While I was young I spent a lot of time working alongside my father or mother."
4. "I came from a close-knit, happy family."
5. "Some young people are expected to do a lot of work (farm chores, yard work, or part-time job), while others are expected to do very little.  Compared with other youth, how much work would you say you were expected to do during your teen years?"

An examination of these five items indicates that the development of the work ethic is strongly influenced by childhood experiences and expectations.  Those who had a strong believe in the moral importance of work generally came from close-knit families in which children were expected to assume personal responsibilities and parents occasionally worked with the children to make certain the jobs were done.  The question asking about the importance of religion suggests that discipline and self-control are important personal characteristics accompanying family expectations in the development of the work ethic. Thus, family expectations, early work experiences, and discipline appear to be important factors in the development of a strong belief about the importance of hard work and the dignity of labor.

## Interviews with Outstanding Workers.

The dramatic effects of early childhood experiences are also illustrated in the interviews we conducted with outstanding performers. The purpose of the interviews was to identify the characteristics of outstanding workers—what they were like and how they got to be that way. Most of these outstanding performers were considered the best workers in the company. Several mediocre and poor workers were also interviewed to serve as a basis for comparison.

The first question asked in the interviews was, "How work-oriented are you?" All of the outstanding performers replied without hesitation that they were very work-orientated. Work was an important part of their life and provided meaning, fulfillment, and satisfaction for them.

The second question was, "How long have you been that way?" All but three workers said they had been that way all their lives, at least back to their early childhood days. The three exceptions identified periods in adulthood when they made significant changes in their values as a result of changing their environment. The fact that these three had made significant changes as adults shows that even though most values are acquired during childhood, adults can also have significant experiences that alter their values.

The next question focused on the central purpose of the interview: "How did you get to be so work-oriented?" All but the same three said they acquired their strong work orientation from their parents— "It was the way I was raised." Fathers were mentioned most frequently as the major source of work values. None of the outstanding workers could remember a specific learning experience when someone undertook to teach them the value of work. Instead, they reported numerous small episodes when they observed their parents at work, when they worked alongside their parents, or when their parents gave them a responsibility and supervised them as they performed it. One worker described how he watched his father work. He remembered how important it was to his father to do things right. His father was a carpenter and if the door he had hung did not swing right, he would rip it out and start over again. His motto was "If you do it right the first time, you won't have to come back and do it again," and he repeated it frequently, hoping to influence his children.

Another worker described how her experiences during childhood shaped her philosophy about work. She came from a large family of eleven children, mostly girls, and recalled how her mother would awaken the family early every morning, particularly during the summer, and send them out to work in the garden while it was still cool. Although her family did not own a farm, she spent many hours working in their family garden or in the fields of nearby farmers. She said that it was very important to her mother for the children to be happy and united in their work. The children who were faster in harvesting or weeding their own rows were expected to help those who were behind. One of her mother's favorite sayings was, "He who helps his brother to the end of the row gets there." This woman was the office manager of a small electronics firm, and hanging on the wall by her desk was another one of her mother's favorite sayings, "Be happy in your work."

## A Profile of Outstanding Workers

The experiences described by these outstanding workers had several common themes. The first and most significant theme was the importance of discipline and obedience. Almost all of the outstanding workers indicated that their parents were loving and kind. But they believed in strict discipline and demanded obedience from their children. When told to do something, the children were expected to do it without a lot of complaining or whining.

A second theme was the importance of working and performing family chores. Everyone was expected to work. Even young children were assigned chores and expected to do them. During unstructured events, such as family outings, everyone was expected to pitch in and help. If there was a job to be done, everyone was expected to help without being asked.

A third theme was the importance of religion. Most of the

outstanding workers indicated that a belief in God and regular church attendance were fundamental parts of their early lives. Church attendance had decreased for some in their early adult lives, but their early religious training was still the basis by which they made moral and ethical decisions about such things as divorce, abortion, bribery, and pornography. After they became parents, religion reemerged as an important foundation for teaching children moral values.

A fourth theme was the importance of doing the "right" thing even if it was unpopular or difficult. Several outstanding workers described experiences involving some form of self-denial where they did what they did because it was the right thing to do even if it was not pleasurable. In fact, certain activities such as heavy work and body conditioning were physically painful, but they did them because they were the right things to do. Some workers obviously derived great satisfaction in accomplishing difficult tasks that they thought would benefit themselves or others. Their lives seemed to be guided by principles of what is right and wrong rather than what is fun and pleasurable.

A fifth theme was frugality. Since many outstanding workers had been raised in poverty, frugality was a necessity. But even those who were not poor accepted thrift and conservation as important personal values. Turning off lights, fixing leaking water faucets, wearing clothes long after the first signs of wear, and avoiding impulse buying or the purchase of convenience items were well-ingrained characteristics.

The sixth theme was the importance of personal responsibility and individual effort to achieve success. Outstanding performers rejected the idea that success is mainly determined by luck, chance, or who you know. Instead, they believed that their success was determined by how much effort they put into their work and the amount of skill and experience they had acquired.

These six characteristics seemed to be especially descriptive of outstanding performers. Mediocre and poor performers occasionally described themselves as possessing some of these characteristics, but there was usually a dramatic difference in the frequency and intensity with which these characteristics were reported by outstanding performers.

## What Are Your Work Values?

As a general rule, parents teach what they are. Everything you do and say has an influence on your children and contributes to their values and attitudes. Furthermore, every parent-child interaction is also a value exchange. Although some interactions are more profound than others, everything you do and say reflects your values by revealing your attitudes and underlying assumptions. Your values get transmitted to your children even when you are not trying to transmit them. Political and religious values, for example, are transmitted by your conversations even though you do not consciously discuss politics or religion. The reality many parents overlook is the fact that they cannot choose to not influence their children's values. Children acquire most of their parents' values whether the parents want them to or not.

Some parents say they do not want to influence their children's values; they want their children to decide for themselves what is right and wrong. One father expressed the following absurd position: "We want our child to establish his own values, therefore we do not plan to talk with him about values until he is sixteen. By then he will be old enough to decide whether what we say is right or wrong and can choose for himself." This father is deluded and mistaken. By the time his son is sixteen, he will have developed a well-defined value system. Altering this basic value structure at this point in life would require a very powerful, confrontive experience. Therefore, parents need to be actively involved in shaping the values and attitudes of young children. Since the values they teach will reflect the values they believe, parents should carefully assess their own values.

What are your work values? The next chapter explains how

to teach work values to children, but before you read it, examine your own values. How do you feel about work? How important is it to you to take pride in your work? Is your behavior consistent with your values? Do you practice what you preach?

To help you assess you personal values about work, read each of the following statements and decide whether you agree or disagree with them. Remember, there are no right or wrong answers here; these statements measure your personal values about work and you are free to express your own feelings. You may have very strong and clearly defined values about work as a result of spending many hours thinking about these issues. Most people, however, have rather loosely defined feelings about some of these issues and need to spend more time thinking about them. After you read each statement, decide whether you agree or disagree with it and then how strongly you agree or disagree. If you strongly disagree, circle a 1; if you strongly agree, circle a 7. If you slightly agree, circle a 5; and so forth.

|  | | Strongly disagree | | Neutral | | | Strongly agree |
|---|---|---|---|---|---|---|---|
| 1. | Being a diligent worker makes you a better person. | 1 | 2 | 3 | 4 | 5 | 6 | 7 |
| 2. | A good indication of your personal worth is how well you do your job. | 1 | 2 | 3 | 4 | 5 | 6 | 7 |
| 3. | Rich people should feel an obligation to work, even if they do not need to. | 1 | 2 | 3 | 4 | 5 | 6 | 7 |
| 4. | Work should be one of the most important parts of a person's life. | 1 | 2 | 3 | 4 | 5 | 6 | 7 |

| | | Strongly disagree | | Neutral | | Strongly agree | | |
|---|---|---|---|---|---|---|---|---|---|

5. An unproductive worker is not loyal to his or her country.    1  2  3  4  5  6  7

6. I would quit working and try to enjoy life if I inherited a lot of money.*    1  2  3  4  5  6  7

7. A worker should do a decent job whether or not the supervisor is around.    1  2  3  4  5  6  7

8. Workers should feel a sense of pride in their work.    1  2  3  4  5  6  7

9. Even if you dislike your work you should do your best.    1  2  3  4  5  6  7

10. People should enjoy their work.    1  2  3  4  5  6  7

11. Getting recognition for my own work is important to me.    1  2  3  4  5  6  7

12. There is nothing wrong with doing a poor job at work if you can get away with it.*    1  2  3  4  5  6  7

*Reverse the score on these items before averaging your test scores.

After responding to these items you can average your answers to calculate two scores. (Before adding your scores together, however, you need to reverse the scoring on items six and twelve: a 7 becomes a 1, a 6 becomes a 2, a 5 becomes a 3, and so forth.) The first six statements measure a value called the moral importance of work. This value refers to the extent to which people believe they have a moral obligation to have a job that provides a useful product or service for society. In a survey of over 3,000 American workers, the average moral importance of work score was 4.82.

The last six items measure the value of pride in craftsmanship, which refers to the extent to which individuals believe they have an obligation to perform their jobs well. The average score for 3,000 American workers was 6.23, and you can compare your score with this average. This number indicates that most American workers believe they should do an excellent job regardless of whether their supervisor is around or whether they like their work.

Whether your scores are higher or lower than the average American worker is not as important as the justification and reasoning you used in responding to these items. To help you think more clearly about your personal values, consider the following questions.

Does working hard make you a better person or simply a workaholic? Obviously, working hard all the time can be carried to an extreme, yet most people believe that being a diligent worker is a positive attribute of good character.

Is the quality of your work a good indication of your personal worth? This question can't be answered very satisfactorily until you decide how you measure an individual's personal worth. A hospital administrator expressed the following philosophy: "I don't have any greater personal worth than anyone else. Any skid-row bum has as much personal worth as I do. I may be of greater value to the hospital, but I don't have any more personal worth than a skid-row bum." However, the nine members of the hospital's board of directors did not agree with this administrator's egalitarian philosophy. Their moral importance of work scores averaged 6.60, and their pride in craftsmanship scores averaged 6.88.

This same egalitarian philosophy was expressed by a sixteen-year-old who was sitting by me on a lengthy airplane ride. Her father, who sat on the other side of her, expressed a significantly different point of view, however. He argued very tenaciously that the personal worth of people was determined by their contribution to society. The people who have the greatest personal worth, according to the father, were those who helped to build society and make it a better place. The rapists, murderers, and prisoners, he argued, not only failed to make a positive contribution to society but had negative personal worth because of their destructive influence. Seeing the diversity in the opinions between the daughter and the father helped me to appreciate the conflict that existed between them. A year earlier the daughter had run away from home and had only recently returned at the pleading of the father. The purpose of the trip was to spend a week together on the ski slopes of Utah. They were hoping to build a better relationship between them. As we rode together, I invited each of them to respond to my questionnaire measuring work values, and we had a fairly lengthy and intense discussion. I thought it was a very enlightening discussion where meaningful ideas were freely shared. But, near the end of the flight, when the father excused himself to go to the restroom, the daughter looked at me very seriously and asked if her father had paid me to accompany them on the flight.

An insightful way to ask whether individuals believe they have a moral obligation to work is to ask whether they would continue working if they inherited a lot of money, or if rich people should feel an obligation to work even if they don't need to. (No doubt many of us would like to face that dilemma.) On one hand, it can be argued that rich people have no obligation to work and that they should feel perfectly free to enjoy life by traveling and spending money however they choose. Some people even argue that the only obligation rich people should feel is the obligation to bolster the economy by spending their money. On the other hand, it can be argued that rich people have more responsibility to work than the average citizen because of the wealth they possess. Their work does not necessarily have to be a paid occupation, but it must be some sort of useful activity that provides a valuable product or service to society. Most rich people spend time investing their money, but should their contributions be more than simply managing their investments?

Who are the rich people, and how did they get to be so rich? Although we would like to think they became wealthy by saving their money and investing it wisely, no one becomes a millionaire by working for an hourly wage and saving money. Most of the truly wealthy people in our society inherited their wealth, received it through luck, or capitalized on the labors of others.

Most Americans claim that loyalty to your country has nothing to do with whether you are a productive worker. You can be a true-blue, flag-waving American regardless of whether you are an outstanding performer or a careless, sloppy, and incompetent worker. Some people even feel a bit irritated being asked to answer this question. It was added to our questionnaire after we made the decision to extend our research into some of the Asian countries, especially Japan, Taiwan, and Singapore. Several people suggested that most Asian employees have very strong feelings about the importance of doing a good job and that careless work is evidence of a lack of loyalty. Although very few Americans believe that being an unproductive worker is evidence of disloyalty, most Asian employees do. In Singapore, government-sponsored publicity campaigns claim that the country's economic survival depends in part upon the loyal contribution of productive employees.

Thinking about these issues should help you clarify your own personal values and assess their importance. Parents who have a clear understanding of their own values are more successful in teaching them to their children. Pride in craftsmanship and a commitment to excellence are important values for children to learn.

By teaching these values, parents help their children achieve greater personal fulfillment and a high quality of life. The study of outstanding workers indicated that these people were happy, enthusiastic individuals who possessed a contagious zest for living. The foundation for a meaningful and fulfilling life begins in the home as parents help their children learn obedience, self-discipline, and self-respect.

## Summary

*A survey of adult employees found that the best predictors of which individuals would have strong work values were (a) whether their family expected them to perform well on the job. (b) whether religion was important to them, (c) whether they came from a close-knit, happy family, and (d) whether they were expected to work as a child.*

*Interviews with outstanding workers revealed that the following characteristics were important during their earlier lives: discipline and obedience, family chores, religion, doing what is "right" as a matter of principle, frugality, and personal responsibility.*

*Parents teach their values to their children both consciously and unintentionally by everything they do and say; therefore, they need to clarify their own values.*

# 6

# Teaching Responsibility Through Work

One of your most valuable opportunities for teaching responsibility is when you teach your children to work. Numerous opportunities for teaching personal responsibility are presented when you assign family chores to your children, supervise their work, and evaluate their performance. Parents can also use other useful activities to teach responsibility, such as music lessons, schoolwork, sports, church callings, service projects, and caring for grandparents. Children learn responsibility by accepting assignments and learning to work independently. Although childhood and adolescence should be happy years when children learn to play, they also need to learn that life consists of more than just pleasure and self gratification. When there is work to do, children need to learn they are expected to do their share. They don't need to work all the time, but they should have responsibilities consistent with their age and ability.

## Assigning Family Chores

The father of two teenage boys lamented. "When I was a kid I was raised on a farm. I had to milk cows morning and night every day of the year. During the summer I weeded corn and hauled hay. I enjoyed working with my dad and my uncle and learned how to work. But what can I do with my boys? I work in an office and there is no way they can work with me. They can't even get a job in the neighborhood. Shouldn't I be teaching them to work the same as I learned to work?"

The scoutmaster of a Boy Scout troop complained of limited job opportunities for his Scouts. "The *Boy Scout Handbook* says that a Boy Scout is supposed to pay his own way. That takes a pretty decent job when you total all the costs for uniforms, equipment, and travel. I have only one boy in my troop who makes that kind of money, and he has a paper route. The other kids have to beg from their parents because they can't earn enough through odd jobs."

The first requirement for teaching children responsibility is to have work for them to do. Most communities provide numerous educational and recreational experiences for young people, but inadequate work opportunities. Consequently, one of your first responsibilities is to help your children find work to do.

**Parents need to provide meaningful work experiences for children**. Regardless of your child's age, you will need to be actively involved in helping the child find work. This responsibility is particularly important for teenagers—finding a job can be extremely frustrating for both teenagers and parents. The problem is not a lack of work; there will always be plenty of work to do. The problem is a lack of jobs. Someone needs to organize the work and create the jobs. Opportunities to beautify and repair homes, yards, and gardens are almost limitless. If given in the proper way, there is also no end to the amount of useful service that can be extended to others, especially to older people. These activities are not "make-work" projects; it is meaningful work that benefits the child, the recipient, and society.

Young people who have enough initiative can create their own jobs, and some of them do. But most children do not have the foresight to know what they can do or the experience to know how to go about doing it. Consequently, parents need to use their own initiative to create tasks for their children. Some parents have recognized this problem and have ingeniously created rather fascinating jobs. Some jobs are clever and some are profitable, even though they almost always entail added work for the parents. But if you want to teach your child how to work, you must be willing to spend the necessary time and effort to create meaningful work opportunities.

**Tasks for toddlers.** Young children don't need very many work assignments, and ample jobs are usually available within the home. Young children should be expected to do more and more to take care of themselves, such as feeding themselves, dressing themselves, picking up their toys, making their own beds, and cleaning their own room. As they continue to mature they should gradually begin performing tasks that help the family, such as taking dirty clothes to the laundry, setting and clearing the table, washing the dishes, cleaning the house, and working in the yard.

The philosophy that should guide parents as they assign tasks to small children is helping them become self-sufficient. Obviously young children need to be fed and dressed by adults. But as they become older, children should begin to assume these responsibilities. Likewise, when they are young someone has to pick up their toys and make their beds. But these responsibilities, too, should be accepted by children as they become old enough. Learning that each person is responsible for his own welfare and well-being is an important insight that children should begin to learn at an early age.

Working with small children provides parents an excellent opportunity to teach them how to get a job done. The biggest challenge is being patient. Parents could clean the playroom or clear the dishes in a fraction of the time it takes to assist the child. But they need to be patient and remember that teaching responsibility is more important than getting the job done. "He who can do ten men's work is not as valuable as he who can get ten men to work."

Although young children should be involved in performing household chores and taking care of themselves, they should not be burdened with a large number of tasks. The "work" of a child is to learn how to play and be happy. Learning how to communicate with others and how to be a good friend are important responsibilities that could almost be viewed as a full-time job.

**Household chores**. By the time children are ten or twelve, they are usually old enough to perform more tasks than are found in most homes with an average-sized lot. At this age parents need to help children find meaningful jobs. A meaningful job is especially desirable during the summer months when children have a lot of time. With a little ingenuity, parents and children can generate some creative ideas. The jobs could be for profit, such as working for a neighbor with a larger house or lot, working on a farm, or making novelty items to sell. The jobs can also be for service, such as helping a community or church organization, tutoring younger students, or helping older people. The jobs can even be designed for learning, such as converting part of the backyard into a garden, raising pets, building model airplanes, or other hobbies.

Many ingenious ideas have been novel but effective. One young girl started with a window flower box and turned a bay window area into a vegetable garden interspersed with flowers. A father bought the vacant lot across the street and coached his two teenage sons as they built a home on it. With a few borrowed tools, a thirteen-year-old boy set up a bicycle repair shop at the back of the family carport. Using a variable pricing schedule, he was able to make a little money and a lot of friends Once a teenager was willing to deliver it, a church leader began sending weekly newsletters to church members. Two siblings earned several hundred dollars each summer selling melons they grew in the vacant lot behind their home.

An important criterion in creating jobs for children is that the jobs must be meaningful. That is, they should provide a useful product or service for someone. Make-work projects are easy to construct; they fill time; they might require physical exertion; and they may be similar to productive jobs in many ways. But children who believe their tasks are no more meaningful than digging holes and filling them again cannot get very enthusiastic about their work or feel very good about it. Therefore, the tasks should be meaningful.

**Parents must assume the responsibility for making jobs meaningful. Jobs are meaningful only if the parents have given them meaning.** The meaningfulness of a job is primarily created by parents through the process of induction (or teaching). No job is inherently meaningful for a young child. Even some of the most obvious jobs, like washing dirty dishes and making beds, are not obviously meaningful to young children. Although you may think it's rather silly now, you can probably remember when you asked yourself, why do we need to wash the dishes after every meal? They just get dirty again when we use them. Why not just leave them on the table and continue eating from them? One young lad even suggested a better idea: he proposed leaving a little food on his plate, placing it on the floor for the dog to lick clean, and then putting it back on the table.

To a little kid, this might seem like a good idea—it even accomplishes two jobs at once. But as parents, you can offer several good reasons why both of these ideas are bad ideas—eating from dirty plates is not very appetizing, the food would not taste as good, and the bacteria growing in leftover food would make you sick. These are good, rational reasons why washing dishes is an important and meaningful job. But can you provide equally persuasive reasons why beds should be made each morning? Probably not, but you don't need to provide crystal-clear justifications that are as profound as "You'll get sick and die if you don't." In fact, many times a very simple explanation is all you need to provide, such as: it makes the house look better, or it makes others happy, or it preserves something and makes it last longer. Children will feel that an activity is meaningful even if you only say, "It's very important to me and I would really like to have you do it."

If parents have carefully decided why they want the child to perform a task, there is usually a reasonable rationale behind the assignment. Many parents expect their children to obey them simply because they are the parents. But if parents will explain why a job is important, the child will feel a greater motivation to perform it.

**Children should not always be asked to perform the most unpleasant jobs**. One mistake parents often make in assigning jobs to children is giving them the unpleasant jobs that the parents do not want to do. If children see that they are always being asked to do the dirty, miserable, and unpleasant chores, they are justified in being unhappy. It violates their sense of fairness. If a father dislikes cleaning the doghouse, he can safely conclude that his son would not like it any better. Likewise, if a mother assigns her daughter to clean the bathroom because she dislikes cleaning around the toilet, she has only transferred her misery onto her, not eliminated it. This does not mean that doghouses and bathrooms should not be cleaned, or that parents should always clean them. Doghouses and bathrooms need to be cleaned occasionally, and they will not clean themselves. Someone has to do the unpleasant jobs. What you need is an alternative procedure so that your child does not feel mistreated and abused.

There are several strategies for handling unpleasant tasks. A simple procedure that seems intuitively fair is sharing the task, such as, "I'll clean the bathroom this week and you do it next week." Another alternative is a negotiated settlement. Here, one person may agree to do the unpleasant task all the time in exchange for some other incentive. The trade-off could entail more money, more privileges, or less work in some other area. For example, "I'll clean the basement each week (requiring ninety minutes ) if you'll clean the doghouse (which only requires thirty minutes.)" Another alternative is to work together and both get the unpleasant job done. Working together has the advantage of providing social interaction and emotional support while the task is being done. Therefore, working together makes the task a little less unpleasant.

**Teenage employment.** At the age of fourteen or fifteen, most teenagers would like to have a real job working for a real employer. At this age they are not ready to be treated as a fully mature adult, and their jobs need to be tailored to their physical size and intellectual maturity. Nevertheless, most fourteen- and fifteen-year-old youth are sufficiently mature to accept a regular job. Furthermore, most teenagers at this age are desirous of having some type of employment to help them establish their individuality and to create a feeling of independence. By the age of sixteen or seventeen, this desire for independence and an opportunity to demonstrate their maturity often becomes such an overwhelming passion that teenagers feel compelled to express it in one form or another. If they can't do it constructively through employment, athletics, or hobbies, they may choose to do it destructively through other forms of rebellion.

The greatest obstacle preventing fourteen- and fifteen-year-olds from working is not that they don't want to work or that their parents are not willing to let them. The problem is finding something to do. Inadequate work opportunities for teenagers is a societal problem that has evolved over the past two centuries. This problem will not be solved until there is a change in the Fair Labor Standards Act, which prohibits most employment opportunities for fourteen- and fifteen-year-olds. Although some jobs are available for this age group, the number is clearly inadequate; and parents need to be creative to find meaningful volunteer work or paid employment for their children.

A companion problem is too much work. A full-time job that

teaches teenagers how to produce and how to be responsible is very desirable during the summer vacation. But, during the school year, most teenagers who have jobs spend far too many hours working. Students who work 20 or more hours per week miss valuable opportunities to participate in meaningful activities at school, at home, and at church. Part time work can be valuable, but it must be limited. The evidence indicates that students who work part time actually perform better in school than those who do not work.[22] BUT, they should not work more than 10 to 15 hours per week and they often need some flexibility in their schedules.

Teenagers ought to consider the possibility of working with an employer to create a new position specifically for them. Employers often find themselves involved in trivial matters that could be effectively delegated to others, but they don't have anyone to delegate them to. If a responsible teenager demonstrated sufficient initiative, the employer would probably be anxious to hire the teenager. This would allow employers to make more effective use of their time.

Some teenagers have been remarkably successful in creating their own jobs. A high school student interested in becoming an engineer contacted a small engineering firm and requested a job. The student was told that the firm did not have any job openings and, furthermore, that they did not hire high school-age students. The student persisted, however, and asked one of the engineering partners if he would be willing to examine his resume, since he was interested in engineering. One of the senior partners agreed to spend five minutes reviewing the student's resume the following day. When the student met with the managing partner, he emphasized his interest in becoming a design engineer and expressed his desire to do anything he could to learn more about the engineering profession. After a few minutes, the managing partner was sufficiently impressed by the dedication of the student that he decided to create a temporary summer job. The engineering firm discovered that this student performed many of the trivial, repetitive chores that prevented managers from doing more significant responsibilities.

# Supervising the Work

To develop good work habits, children need to be carefully supervised and parents need to be good supervisors. In fact, children usually need more supervision than parents think; but parents should also avoid hovering over their children directing every motion unless they need special assistance.

What children need is effective supervision. The value of an effective supervisor is even greater in the home than in industry. Parents are the unsung heroes of our society, and more credit and recognition needs to be given them—especially to the countless mothers who work in the home raising the family. Mothers who manage a home should think of themselves as the world's greatest group of managers. Very few managers in industry make as many managerial decisions each day as the typical mother in the home. The following principles should help parents supervise their children's work.

**When delegating work assignments, parents need to establish a psychological contract.** A *psychological contract* is an agreement with the child that describes what is to be done and explains the standards of expected performance. The major purpose of the contract is to develop individual responsibility and initiative. Effectively delegating jobs to children involves three major steps:

1. The first step consists of "writing the contract," in other words, developing the agreement with the child. The contract should specify what is to be done, how soon it must be completed, and a standard of performance to determine if it was done adequately.

2. Second, the contract should provide for periodic reviews of some sort, such as weekly progress reports, inspections, or even written reports.

3. Finally, the contract should call for a final accountability so the child anticipates from the beginning the time when he or she will report on the completion of the job. If the job is an

ongoing job that is never "finished," the accountability is incorporated in the periodic reviews.

If these three steps are done properly, the chances will be greater that the job will get done, the parents will be happy, and the child will have a positive orientation towards work. The contract does not need to be a formal document, nor must it be written. However, there are advantages to having a written description of the responsibilities available on a bulletin board or some other visible place, such as a bathroom mirror, the kitchen wall, or a bookcase in the bedroom. Written descriptions help parents and children remember the important parts of the contract, and it reduces the disagreement between parents and children about the terms of the agreement.

The following are some examples of simple contracts:

- "Within an hour after dinner and before you get involved in anything else, we'd like you to clean the kitchen (or clear the table, wash the dishes, wipe of the counter, dry the dishes, or put them away). At our family home evening you can report how well you've done the job."

- "The garage needs to be cleaned sometime this week. The tools need to be organized on the tool bench and the bicycles need to be put in their places. The floor needs to be swept and hosed. After you've finished, let me know."

**In delegating work assignments, parents should try to delegate the outcomes they expect rather than the activities.** When the contract is written, parents need to decide whether they should delegate the final outcome they expect (such as a clean bedroom) or the activities that lead to the outcome (such as make your bed, straighten the books on the shelf, pick up your clothes, put your shoes in the closet, close the closet doors). It is preferable for parents to delegate the outcome when the child is sufficiently mature and can accept the responsibility for it. Mature children will use their own creativity and initiative to decide which activities are needed, and parents are freed from the necessity of constantly monitoring their performance. If something unusual occurs, a mature child responsible for the outcome will handle the situation himself, while a child who is performing a prescribed sequence of activities will wait for updated directions.

Young children have a short attention span and short memories. It is easy for them to forget daily responsibilities, and for several years they might need to be reminded to do their chores. Parents can help children remember their jobs by arranging the activities in a sequence. For example, a child could be taught to follow a patterned sequence, such as make his bed, get dressed, pick up his clothes, brush his teeth, and then take the dirty clothes to the laundry room. A chart with pictures showing the sequence of activities could help the child remember each step in the sequence.

Even when their chores are all arranged in a sequence, however, they might forget the entire sequence and leave the room without making their beds. It would be nice if children always remembered their chores, but they can become easily engrossed in other activities. Therefore, you ought to accept the fact that you will have to remind them again and again. Rather than feeling distraught by the times they forget, try to find solace in the few times they remember.

**Develop commitment and responsibility through the exercise of personal choice**. Consider the following ingredients: (1) a lawn that is tall and needs to be cut weekly; (2) a fourteen-year-old boy who is physically healthy and capable of mowing the lawn; and (3) a father who has decided that his fourteen-year-old son should mow the lawn because he has ample time and there is no reasonable excuse why he should not mow it.

Does it matter how these ingredients get mixed together? In other words, does it matter how the contract gets established?

Yes, how the assignment is made will largely determine the boy's personal commitment to mow the lawn. Personal choice is essential in establishing the contract. The child should personally decide to accept the task and agree to do it. The success of each step in establishing the contract hinges on the extent to which the child decides to do it. To obtain personal commitment, the child should be allowed to make a personal decision at each step, even if the decision has been predetermined or is largely out of his control. There is a subtle, but significant, difference between telling a child what to do and getting him to agree to do it.

When a child is told what to do and then forced to do it, either by threat of punishment or by promise of reward, he tends to have no personal commitment. He is doing the task because he was told to do it, not because he is willing or has agreed to do it. He is not exercising his own personal agency. He does not "own" the task; in other words, he is not responsible for how it is done, nor is he responsible for the result.

When a child agrees to perform a task, however, he tends to develop a feeling of personal commitment. Accomplishing the task becomes an integral part of his life. He "owns" the task; he is responsible for its success or failure. His self-evaluation and his self-esteem are influenced by how he evaluates his performance. Personal choice leads to commitment and responsibility.

Obviously, these are two extreme positions that overstate the subtle differences between allowing or not allowing a choice. One or two unique opportunities to make a choice will not make a dramatic change in the development of personal commitment. Personal commitment is not easily developed or quickly destroyed by a few specific instances in which a child does or does not agree to perform a task. Attributes of character, such as personal commitment, develop over a long period of time and demand a lot of persistence from parents and teachers.

So what should the father do when he assigns the son to mow the lawn? Along with everything else the father says in the process of assigning the task, he should at some point ask the son to do it and wait for an answer. The question can be a simple inquiry such as "How about it?" or "Will you do it?" or "What do you say?" but it should not be so casual or so quickly passed over that the child does not consciously think about it.

What should parents do if the child says no? This can be a difficult situation requiring tremendous skill and sensitivity on the part of parents. There may be times when the parents decide unalterably that no is not an acceptable answer, and the child simply must perform the task. Parents have their own set of punishments and rewards for such conditions, but before parents bring the heavy hand of authority crashing down they would be wise to learn whether the child has any reasonable cause to say no. A little understanding and some patient explanation can usually achieve marvelous results. But even when all rational logic fails and the threats of punishments or promises of rewards leave the child with no alternative but to agree, it is still a good idea to again ask if he is willing to do it. It may be an extremely small step in the direction of greater personal commitment, but it is at least a step in the right direction.

**Tasks should not be assigned thoughtlessly or in a careless way.** Parents err when they ask children to do a task before the parents have adequately considered it. If parents get in the habit of thoughtlessly assigning tasks off the top of their heads, children get in the habit of not paying attention. The father of a nine-year-old thought that a bright spring day would be an excellent time to teach his son how to work by having him assist in making repairs on the sprinkler system. As the father operated the shovel to dig up the broken sprinkler heads, the boy stood idly and watched. Once the repairs got under way, however, the boy faced an endless barrage of instructions. After responding to several requests to "get me this" or "bring me that,"the father gave the instruction "go get the hammer." Before the boy could return with the hammer, the father used the back of a wrench for a hammer. As the boy was returning with the hammer, the father issued another directive to turn on the sprinkler valve. Ignoring the latest command, the boy continued to bring the hammer, which provoked the father to raise his voice: "Go turn on the sprinkler right now!" With some surprise the boy explained, "I'm bringing you the hammer," and was even more surprised to hear the father say, "I don't need it, put it back. I want you to go turn on the sprinkler."

When children are asked to accomplish tasks in a thoughtless, careless way, they quickly learn that the less often they are around, the less they get asked to do. This is true for big jobs as well as for little requests such as "turn off the sprinkler," "bring me a knife," and "get me the hammer." A lot of little requests, one after another, have a way of adding up to a big discomfort. When the boy got to the sprinkler valve, he decided not to take the hammer back because there was a good chance he would be asked to get it again. Consequently, he left the hammer by the sprinkler valve and slipped away to play with a neighbor next door. "When Dad starts working in the yard," he thought to himself, "it just isn't safe to be around." Later the father expressed his disappointment that his son had not stayed and worked with him. The father wanted his son to learn how to work. The son had, in fact, learned a valuable lesson: he learned that when he works with his dad, he gets asked to do a lot of trivial jobs and he may get yelled at even when he's doing them. In his mind, when Dad starts working in the yard, the safest strategy is to disappear.

Before parents assign a task to a child they ought to ask themselves several questions: "Do I really want this task done, or is it just a wild idea I happened to think about?" "How long will it reasonably take for them to do this task, and will it continue to be important until it is done?" "Have I recently assigned other tasks, and am I making too many requests for them to remember or accomplish?" When a child is asked to get a screwdriver and returns to find that his father has successfully used a dime instead, he not only faces the disappointment of knowing his efforts were worthless but also feels the added humiliation of having to return the screwdriver. Parents need to carefully decide what tasks they want to assign and then assign them with discretion. Taking time to discuss the assignment and why it is important rather than casually mentioning the request as a passing thought communicates a message of significance, importance, and urgency.

**Adequate assistance should be given, but too much assistance can be destructive.** One mother said, "I rely on family chores to teach my children responsibility, but it is not easy for me to be patient. When I become too task-oriented, I try to remind myself that I'm staying home to teach and train my children, not to keep my drawers clean. It's the children that matter; they have to be the focus, not the task."

Getting started is sometimes the most difficult part of the task, and parents can save a lot of time and hassle if they get the task started right. Younger children especially need the kind of help and encouragement that comes, for example, from an adult picking up the first toy and putting it away. Parents occasionally need to work with children to show them how to perform the task and, more importantly, how to be happy in their work.

Many of the jobs that are so simple and uncomplicated for parents to perform are not simple or uncomplicated for children. Parents overlook the inherent difficulty of tasks they have routinely performed for many years. Consequently, they find themselves feeling irritated and disappointed when they observe their children's awkward inefficiency and incompetence. Criticism and harassment at these times are not as useful as patient demonstrations. An adult who has washed dishes several thousand times may feel very frustrated watching a seven-year-old flip water all over with the tail of the dishcloth, try to wipe a counter with the dishcloth wadded into a tight ball, or overflow the sink with dishwater while trying to rinse excess soap from the dishes. The child needs some patient advice on how much soap to use, how to use the dishcloth, and the best process for washing and rinsing.

One of the greatest dangers in giving assistance is that you terminate the contract by usurping responsibility for the task. If you are not careful when you give assistance, you can make your child feel he has been released from the responsibility of accomplishing the task. At the time the contract was written, provisions should have been made for the child to ask for assistance. But if parents take responsibility for the task when giving assistance, they terminate the contract and release the child from the agreement.

Assistance needs to be given in a way that does not terminate the agreement. The responsibility of asking for help and determining what help is needed should remain with the child. This is accomplished when parents say "I can do _____ if you want me to" or "What would you like me to do to help you?" Parents should let the child take the lead in the review process and let the child evaluate his own progress and ask for specific help. Carefully worded questions that cause the child to consider the situation ("If you water only one area each day, will you be able to keep the grass green?") are generally much better than parental evaluations ("You have to remember to water more than one area a day or the grass will die").

The appropriate attitude for you to have in providing assistance for your children is, "I am willing to help you, encourage you, and teach you how to do your job, but you have to ask for help if you want it. This is your job, and if you want me to do something to help, you need to tell me what to do." For example, if you said, "I want you to help me do the dishes," your request has clearly indicated that you are responsible for seeing that the dishes are done. But if you said, "I would like you to do the dishes, and I'm willing to help you if you need me to," you have delegated the responsibility for doing the dishes to the child. There is nothing wrong with helping the child get the job done; in fact, the best way for you to teach your child to take pride in his work and to enjoy working is for you to work alongside him. If you start doing the dishes, however, without asking what he wants you to do, you have now taken over the responsibility for the job. You have told the child he was responsible to see that the job was done, and then in your effort to be helpful, and without his doing anything to deserve it, you have demoted him to the status of an assistant rather than the owner of the job.

**Parents are responsible for providing adequate resources and information to accomplish the job.** To do the job correctly children need adequate training and the proper tools and materials. Many times the problem is not that such materials are unavailable, but that the child does not know which ones to use or where they are. The child might not be very excited about scrubbing off the black scuff marks he made on the floor, but more than lack of motivation is involved in keeping him from removing the marks. To the mother the process is simple: use a rag, cleanser, and water. But the child may not realize that he needs to use cleanser; he may not know where the cleanser is; and he may think a washcloth is the only available rag in the house. When children are young, parents need to assume a large part of the responsibility for providing the resources and training. But after children begin to develop a strong work orientation, they will begin to display greater initiative and creativity in providing their own resources. A good indication of your children's maturity in learning to work will be evidenced by the amount of initiative they display in knowing what needs to be done and how to do it without a lot of detailed instructions.

**Children should be expected to make a final accountability report to review their performance.** The final accountability report is an essential step in delegating and supervising work assignments and should have been planned from the start. When the contract was first established, one of its provisions should have been that the child reports when the job is finished. The report is part of the job; the job isn't completed until the report is made.

Children should assume the responsibility for making the report. If the job is a specific assignment (such as painting a picnic table), the report ought to be made as soon as the task is completed. If the job is an ongoing responsibility (such as washing dishes, mowing lawns, or cleaning one's bedroom), the report ought to be made periodically, such as at a weekly family council meeting.

The final report should never be a negative experience. If the task has been properly assigned and adequate follow-though has been provided, the stage is set for a positive experience. The child should have successfully accomplished the task and will be anxious to report on his or her success and receive praise and recognition for his or her efforts.

However, the child may have failed, and the task might not be successfully completed. The final report can still be a positive experience. The failure will not come as a surprise if the agreement and follow-through steps were properly completed. Yelling, screaming, and scolding will not be necessary or even useful. Instead, parents need to explore with the child the reasons for the failure. If more time is needed, perhaps more time can be provided. If more resources are needed, more resources could be provided. If more training is needed, more training can be provided. If the problem was inadequate motivation, more motivation can be provided. The parents can reemphasize the reasons why the job is important, and they can redesign the child's rewards by providing more rewards for doing the job or denying privileges if the job is not done.

Holding a final accountability report is important, not only because of the positive results that are produced, but also because of the negative effects that are avoided. When a final accountability is not held, there is a clear implication that the task is not important and that the parents are not interested in the child. The final accountability report is an excellent time to positively reinforce the child's efforts.

**Children need accurate feedback on their performance and praise and recognition for their success.** The positive effects of praise and recognition have been clearly shown by countless examples. Perhaps the best rule governing human behavior is this: "People do what they expect to be rewarded for doing." Parents need to learn how to be generous in their praise and recognition. There is no reason for parents to feel uncomfortable or reluctant to express genuine appreciation to their children.

One of the most powerful forms of positive reinforcement is social approval, the acceptance and recognition that comes from important people. Children will do many things to obtain social approval. Young children depend primarily on their parents for social approval, whereas teenagers are more concerned about social approval from their peers. A parent cannot be constantly attentive and recognize all of his or her children's accomplishments. But periodically asking children about their activities and successes can be very reinforcing.

It is important for children to receive honest feedback. Inaccurate information is misleading and keeps them from facing reality. When their performance is good, providing accurate feedback is easy and enjoyable. When performance is poor, however, parents often want to distort the feedback. While children need positive experiences, false information can be more damaging than disappointment. Parents need to develop tactful ways of giving accurate information that does not dwell excessively on the child's mistakes but emphasizes the successes and strengths of the child.

## Summary

*Parents need to provide meaningful work experiences for children. Most jobs are meaningful only if parents give them meaning.*

*Children should not always be asked to perform the most unpleasant jobs.*

*Teenagers who have difficulty finding a job may be able to create their own job.*

*When delegating work assignments, parents need to establish a psychological contract with the child and delegate the outcomes they expect rather than the activities.*

*Commitment and responsibility require the exercise of personal choice.*

*Tasks should not be assigned thoughtlessly. Adequate assistance should be given but too much assistance can be destructive.*

*Parents should provide adequate resources and information to accomplish the job.*

*Children should be expected to make a final accountability report to review their performance. Children need accurate feedback on their performance, and praise and recognition for their successes.*

# 7

# Rewarding
# Good Behavior

People do what they expect to be rewarded for doing. Although this statement sounds too simple to be true, it represents a basic principle explaining human behavior. A knowledge of this principle helps parents understand their children's behavior and appreciate the importance of reinforcing good behavior. Parents should be lavish in their praise and constantly look for opportunities to reinforce good behavior.

## Primary and Secondary Rewards

Newborn infants are much easier to understand than teenagers. When infants are hungry or uncomfortable, the pain will cause them to cry. When they are sleepy they may get irritable for a short time, but if they have the opportunity they will sleep. Eating and sleeping occupy a major part of an infant's life, and for the first few months an infant's behavior is largely determined by *primary* reinforcers. Primary reinforcers refer to rewards that are desirable because of their relationship to the phys-iological needs of the human body. Food and water, for example, are primary reinforcers because they satisfy basic physiological needs and allow us to survive when we are hungry or thirsty. Removing pain is also a primary reinforcer simply because it feels good and makes us more comfortable. If you have a splinter in your finger or a rock in your shoe, you are motivated to get them out. No one had to teach you that removing pain was a positive reinforcement. The removal of pain has always been a positive reinforcer; you were born that way—it was innate. Rest is also a primary reward. When you are sleepy, nothing feels better than being able to go to sleep.

These reinforcers are called primary rewards because they are innate or unlearned. They are reinforcing because they satisfy physiological needs and contribute to the survival of the human body. By understanding primary rewards, parents can understand most of a young infant's behaviors. As a child matures, however, *secondary* rewards become far more important than primary rewards in determining behavior, even though the child still needs to eat and sleep.

Secondary rewards are learned rewards. Unlike primary rewards, they are not innate nor are they directly tied to the phys-iology of the body. Nevertheless, secondary rewards such as praise, recognition, status, money, gold stars, and promotions become powerful motivating forces in our lives. In fact, parents need to begin using secondary rewards very early in a child's life to counter the influence of primary rewards. Sitting in church, for example, gets rather uncomfortable after a while, and young chil-dren like to move around to remove the pain. Parents can use the secondary reward of social approval to get children to sit still for longer periods.

Social approval is one of the strongest reinforcers in the lives of young children. At a very young age they begin to learn that parents approve of certain behaviors but not of others. The social-ization process, in which young children learn how to behave in socially accepted ways, is largely guided by a desire to obtain approval from parents. Children do many things simply to win parental approval. If you are consistent in your expectations, you will find that your children's desires for social approval will cause them to do what you want them to do most of the time.

During a child's teenage years the desire for social approval continues to increase. But at this age the most important approval is not from parents, but from peers. When a child is between the ages of ten and twelve, many parents discover that their child's peers exert a  stronger influence than the parents. Most teenagers deny that their friends have a profound influence on their lives; they think they act independently and decide for themselves. To appreciate how limited their self-proclaimed independence really is, however, they only need to look at the clothes they wear. If their friends wear shirts with little alligators on them, so do they. Many teenagers live in constant fear of being ridiculed for doing something unusual. In fact, peer group approval becomes such a powerful reinforcer that many teenagers do not enjoy their youth. They very seldom reinforce each other, and their tendency to criticize rather than compliment creates serious feelings of personal insecurity.

Secondary reinforcers are acquired by experience—by observing the consequences of our own behavior, from listening to the instructions of parents and teachers, and by observing the behavior of others and learning from their experience. The unique learning opportunities we each experience create a combination of secondary reinforcers that influence our behavior. The values we learn are a form of secondary reinforcer that guides our behavior. The work ethic, for example, is essentially a secondary reinforcer that places a high value on working diligently and performing a good job even though it is physically uncomfortable and requires arduous labor. Similarly, honesty and chastity may become powerful secondary reinforcers that effectively control our behavior even though there are powerful primary reinforcers in the form of candy bars and sexual gratification to tempt us to behave otherwise. When a young couple is sitting in a parked car late at night, there are tempting reinforcers encouraging them to engage in sexual activity that they might later regret. Part of the temptation comes from the desire for primary reinforcement in the form of sexual stimulation, but the greatest temptation comes from the secondary reinforcers associated with the excitement of being liked and desired by another individual. Whether they will participate in improper sexual activity or not will be largely determined by the strength of competing secondary reinforcers, chastity and virtue, and how long they remain in a situation in which more immediate sexual reinforcers are present.

## Immediate Versus Distant Rewards

If people do what they are reinforced to do, then why do people have so much trouble accomplishing some of their cherished goals? Why do smokers have so much trouble trying to quit smoking? Why do students have so much trouble studying to get good grades? Why do overweight people have so much difficulty losing weight? Almost every student has had the following experience and used the same rationalizations: "I wish I could finish my homework. I've got a lot of reading to do for my classes, but it's really boring. Every time I sit down to read, someone invites me to play or visit, or else there's a good program on TV. I want to be a good student, but goofing off is much more fun than studying and the exam is so far away. Why don't I study for that exam? If I don't study I know I'll fail, but goofing off or watching television for just five more minutes probably won't hurt. The problem is that I always put off studying for just a little bit longer."

One of the most useful insights that helps to explain why large reinforcers, such as losing weight, quitting smoking, and passing a course, are ineffective is the following principle: *Our behavior is more easily influenced by small, immediate, and definite reinforcers than it is by large, distant, and uncertain reinforcers.*

The problem is not that getting a  good grade, passing the

course, or getting a high school diploma are unimportant; getting a degree is a large, significant reinforcer. But at a given moment in the life of a student, even though graduation from school is a large reinforcer, it also is rather distant and uncertain. The student says, "I am not going to graduate today, and I don't think a few minutes of goofing off or watching TV will hurt my chances of getting a degree." Goofing off is only a small, momentary reward, but it is immediate and certain.

Since behavior is more easily influenced by small, immediate, and definite reinforcers than by large, distant, and uncertain reinforcers, how can individuals achieve long-term goals? The answer is to bring some of the large reinforcers from the future into the present in the form of small, immediate reinforcers. This process is referred to as *contingency management*. A contingency refers to the relationship between the behavior and the reward. New reinforcement contingencies are created to reward small, specific steps leading to the attainment of a large, distant objective.

The following example illustrates the principle of contingency management. Two high school seniors had a strong desire to play in the symphonic band when they attended college. They knew, however, that unless their musical talent improved significantly they would not have that opportunity. After several weeks of shared confessions in which each admitted how poorly she was doing, they created a plan to monitor each other's performance and reward each other for doing what they wanted to do. Each girl knew that she had to practice faithfully, but they both found that visiting was more fun and they always had something to talk about. They resolved to each give six quarters to a third friend at the beginning of the week, and the only way either girl could get her quarters back was by practicing one hour each day. At the end of the week, any money that was still held by their friend was used to buy treats while they visited. Each girl knew the amount of money was small, and if she didn't practice a full hour each day she would only lose twenty-five cents that day. The greatest reinforcer, however, was knowing that someone else was interested and each girl would be forced to acknowledge that she had failed to meet her self-established goal.

Realizing that small, immediate, and certain reinforcers are much more powerful than large, distant reinforcers should help parents design their reward programs. In teaching children to work and getting them to perform other household chores, parents need to provide small, immediate reinforcers rather than rely on large distant ones. Telling children they will have a great family vacation at the end of the summer if they work hard for a couple of months provides almost no reinforcement. Farmers who hire youth to assist with vegetable and fruit harvesting, for example, find it is far more effective, in spite of the hassle, to pay young people at the end of each day than to wait until the weekend to pay them. Even though they know they will get paid by how many pounds they harvest, young people do not work as enthusiastically when they are paid weekly as when they are paid daily. Small, immediate reinforcers have a large impact on the behavior of everyone, especially children.

## Agency Versus Control

Saying that behavior is determined by the kinds of rewards or punishments associated with it provides a very straightforward principle for understanding human behavior. However, human behavior can still be very difficult to understand because the environment contains both rewards and punishments, and some rewards and punishments are difficult to identify. Students like to receive good grades, but they also like to visit with their friends and sometimes studying is boring. Therefore, it is difficult to predict whether the students will be motivated to study.

Many people object to this principle because they believe it destroys personal agency and human dignity. The idea that behavior is controlled by forces in the environment is called determinism; the concern is that determinism is inconsistent with the idea of personal agency. Indeed, when both ideas are pushed to their extremes, they appear to be basically inconsistent. However, a reasoned analysis of both ideas shows that they are not so inconsistent. The basic concept of personal agency claims that at any given point individuals can choose how they will behave among several alternatives. The basic idea of determinism is that the individual's behavior is determined by forces in the environment, and if these forces are changed the behavior of the individual will change in a corresponding way. Both ideas are true when they are not taken to their extreme positions. Individuals are indeed agents and have the opportunity to choose how they will behave within certain limits. How they have behaved in the past and the conditions they have created for themselves will not entirely determine how they will behave in the future. However, individuals cannot entirely ignore either their past or their present circumstances.

The idea that the environment is totally responsible for determining behavior is called "environmental determinism." One of the major problems with environmental determinism is that it fails to recognize the individual's ability to influence his or her environment. A more insightful understanding of determinism is called "reciprocal determinism." Reciprocal determinism recognizes the influence of the environment on the individual, but also claims that individuals have the opportunity to change and redesign their environment. Thus, individuals influence the environment and the environment influences individuals.

An individual who has chosen in the past not to play tennis cannot expect to suddenly play like a tennis star. On the other hand, suppose you wanted your daughter to be a good tennis player and she didn't even like the sport. If you were sufficiently determined and tactful, you could probably succeed in making her an excellent tennis player by carefully constructing an environment that induced her to spend considerable time practicing tennis. By making tennis practicing convenient and attractive, you would probably succeed. To do so you may want to buy her the best tennis equipment, build a tennis court in your own backyard, arrange for enthusiastic tennis players to spend a lot of time at your home, get her friends to spend a lot of time on your tennis court practicing tennis, and perhaps even arrange for them to take tennis lessons so that your daughter has to improve in order to hold her own. For family vacations you could visit several of the major tennis championships, arrange to meet some of the professional tennis players, and even interact with them socially. At some point you should obviously stop and ask yourself why you really want to do all of this, but if having your daughter be a good tennis player is that important to you, there are many things you could do to structure the environment so she would be highly rewarded for doing the things that would lead her to become a good tennis player.

Although behavior is greatly influenced by the environment, it is important to realize that you can change and alter your environment. Once you realize how heavily the environment influences your behavior, you ought to be smart enough to use it to your advantage. If you don't like what you are doing, you are free to change your environment to help you do better. If I had a tennis court in my backyard and I found myself spending too much time playing tennis, I could take down the net and replace it with patio furniture that would have to be moved every time I wanted to play tennis. Or I could give my tennis racket to my neighbor and have him require me to check it out or rent it every time I wanted to play tennis. Most people are able to control their behavior without taking such drastic steps. Nevertheless, it is important to realize the powerful influence the environment has on behavior and to realize that we can change the environment in predictable and desirable ways to obtain better behavior if we want to badly enough.

Sometimes parents discover that their children are acquiring undesirable behaviors. The onset of these undesirable behaviors can often be traced to a new group of associates either at school, in the neighborhood, or at work. With a little coaching and encouragement, parents can usually enlighten their children and insulate them from the negative influence of their environment. If the environmental influence is too great, however, parents may need to transfer their children into a different peer group.

## How to Reward Good Behavior

Three important principles are involved in rewarding good behavior; these principles are equally appropriate for both adults and children. If you think you already know how to reward good behavior and learning these principles is a waste of time, try the following experiment that a father performed with his three children. This father didn't think all three principles were necessary and a broad "Thanks for everything you do," was entirely adequate. According to a prearranged plan, he expressed appreciation to each of his three children individually in the presence of his wife. The father's comment was a simple statement of appreciation: "I just want you to know how much I appreciate everything you do." After he made the comment and left, his wife asked the child why the father had expressed appreciation. The ten-year-old replied, "I guess he must be upset because I didn't get the dishes done like I was supposed to." The thirteen-year-old replied, "I don't know; I guess he was just feeling sentimental." The fifteen-year-old said, "Who knows what he meant. I don't think he understands what's going on around here."

*Describe the desired behavior.* The first principle of rewarding good behavior is to describe the desired behavior in specific terms. Expressing appreciation in general, unspecified terms fails to communicate what the person did right and often appears insincere. In most situations the specific description does not need to be very long or eloquent: "You did a good job washing the dishes; I noticed that you even wiped off the counter and the top of the stove." "I see you took all of the dirty clothes out of the hamper and down to the laundry room before breakfast." "When I was in the basement I noticed that you had changed the light bulb in the fruit room." These statements are not elaborate, but they clearly describe the specific behavior.

***Explain why it was helpful.*** After the appropriate behavior
has been described, you need to indicate why it was helpful.
Sometimes the reason is obvious, but even then it usually helps to
explain why again. These explanations are particularly useful in
helping individuals internalize positive work values. For example, when you tell a child, "You did a good job washing the dishes, wiping off the counter, and cleaning the stove," he can still say
to himself, "So what? I'm glad I've finished with that lousy job."
However, if you add, "That really makes our kitchen look nice,
and it makes our home a lot better," the child begins to internalize the importance of doing a good job washing the dishes. The
explanation also helps the child understand why the job is necessary and why it must be done in a particular fashion: "By getting
the clothes down to the laundry room before breakfast, I can get
the first load of laundry started while we eat."

***Express appreciation.*** The third step in rewarding good performance is simply expressing appreciation. Again, this expression does not have to be elaborate or eloquent. A simple "Thanks"
or "I appreciated it" may be all that is necessary. "When I was in
the basement I noticed that you changed the light bulb in the fruit
room. Now we don't have to grope around in the dark trying to
find what we're after. Thanks for changing it."

## Positive Reward Programs

Parents have designed an enormous number of programs for
monitoring their children's performance and rewarding them. The
following programs are intended to stimulate your thinking and
help you develop a program that will work best for you. There are
no fail-safe programs, and any program you adopt must be adapt-
ed to your family's situation. In choosing a program, remember
the following points. First, all programs require the parents' total
commitment and extensive supervision. Having a successful program requires a lot of time and energy on your part. If you are not
willing to monitor the program, it will not succeed. Second,

design a program that shifts the burden of reporting as much as possible to the child. Older children, especially teenagers, should be capable of assuming the responsibility for performing a task and seeing that it is properly reported and recorded. Third, the program should be designed to reward good performance rather than punish poor performance. Obviously, children who fail to accomplish their tasks may need some form of discipline, but the design of the program should emphasize opportunities for positive reinforcement rather than opportunities for punishment. You should try to make work a pleasant experience, and if the program creates constant strife with your children, try a different program.

*Allowances.* Many children receive a weekly allowance from their parents. Although most allowances are rather modest, some children receive fairly large monthly allowances. A major question is how large the allowance should be. Should the allowance be only one or two dollars per week, or should it be ten to fifteen dollars per week? Parents typically use an allowance schedule that provides more money for older children, such as ten to twenty-five cents per week per year of age.

Another question is whether the allowances should be based on chores. Some parents feel very strongly that children should only receive an allowance if they have contributed by performing household chores. Their allowance is essentially a payment for the work they perform. Other parents feel just as strongly that the allowance should be totally separated from family chores. These parents argue that the allowance is free to the child and represents that individual's share of the family income. These parents claim that the child should feel a personal obligation to assist with family chores without having to be paid.

Both questions—the size of the allowance and whether it should be tied to family chores—are probably not very important. In many respects it doesn't really matter whether the allowance is given for work or for free. The important fact is whether the parents have communicated firm expectations about the child's responsibility to help with family chores. When parents have a clear understanding of the child's responsibility, these expectations get communicated in many ways that are usually much more profound than the differences of a few dollars each week in allowance money. Parents who want to use the allowance to teach their children diligence at work can do so with some advantage, while parents who choose to give allowances freely probably find that it makes only a small difference.

The question regarding the size of the allowance is also not necessarily a very relevant question. The question is not how much money children should receive, but how they should be allowed to spend their money. If children are allowed to spend money on candy, comic books, and other treats, parents may want to reduce the size of their allowance simply to discourage self-indulgence. On the other hand, if children are encouraged to save their money and parents assist them in creating some form of investment or savings account, then a larger allowance may be appropriate. One father who provided a very generous allowance for his son was very pleased with the way his son invested the money and learned the value of savings and investment at an early age. Another generous father, however, was quite disappointed when his son secretly withdrew the majority of his savings and purchased an overpriced motorcycle.

Parents need to teach children how to save and invest money, as well as how to spend it. Just because children have saved their own money does not mean parents should let them spend it however they want. It is not wrong for parents to influence and control a child's expenditures. Indeed, it is irresponsible for parents to think "It's their money; they can spend it how they want" since the parents have a legal responsibility for their children's financial obligations until they reach age 18.

*Tokens*. Some parents have developed elaborate work programs based on some form of tokens or points. One mother, for example, who thought her children were not ready to handle money responsibly gave them "poker" chips each time they completed one of the assigned chores, such as making their beds, cleaning their rooms, picking up their toys, and so forth. The chips could be redeemed for special treats, such as ice cream cones and movies. To use cooperation and peer pressure and get the children to encourage each other in the performance of their jobs, she allowed the children to pool their chips on special occasions.

A similar program is to use a system in which points are assigned to each task. Making the bed, for example, counts for only three points, clearing the dishes will get five points, washing the dishes will get twenty points, and mowing the lawn will bring a full forty-five points. The points could then be exchanged for a variety of desirable activities, such as sleeping at a friend's house, going to movies, and watching television. Children are expected to record on a chart the date the activity was performed and how many points they earned. The parents' job is to review the chart periodically and assign points to unique jobs, such as helping to repair the backyard fence.

*Job charts*. A job chart can be a useful method of assigning family chores and also reminding children about other daily responsibilities, such as brushing their teeth, combing their hair, and making their beds. Some parents construct a chart with each child's name and the days of the week across the top, and the daily activities and other job assignments down the left side. This chart is posted in a prominent place, such as on the refrigerator door or on the wall in the family room, and the children are expected to check the activities they have performed each day. At the end of the week it is easy to see if they failed to help with the dishes, brush their teeth, or complete some other assignment. A convenient time to review the week's performance and assign jobs for the coming week is during a weekly family home evening. The disadvantage of this program, however, is the time it takes to prepare the job chart each week.

A slightly different form of a job chart is a box that has two rows of compartments in which cards can be inserted. Each card describes a job that needs to be performed that day, and at the beginning of the day the parents place the cards in the top rows of their children's boxes. The children look at the assignments in their boxes and move the cards to the bottom row under their names as they complete their job assignments. Pictures on the cards describe the responsibility so that even the young children are able to participate. Many other types of job charts can be constructed for assigning children to tasks and rewarding them for their good performance. The charts do not need to be elaborate, and many times simple gold stars or smiley faces serve quite well to let children know that their performance has been recognized and appreciated.

*Random rewards*. In addition to a regular program of recording completed jobs and recognizing good performance, parents should realize the tremendous motivating power of random rewards. If you question whether random rewards are really powerful, visit a casino and watch people playing bingo or the slot machines. These gamblers know that if they play long enough, they will go broke; if they hit the jackpot, they probably won't go home wealthy—they will simply get to play longer. So why do people play slot machines? The physical act of picking up a coin, putting it in a slot, and pulling a handle does not look very exciting. In fact, most industrial jobs have far greater variety than this simple act. Nevertheless, people play the slots for hour after hour knowing that it's going to cost them as much money as they have allocated, and they are confined in an environment where the noise and cigarette smoke would not meet industrial safety standards. But they continue to play the slots because the rewards come at random. Random rewards, even when they have nothing to do with personal skill and ability, generate an enormous amount of interest and enthusiasm.

One family used a very simple random reward procedure similar to the token program described above. Rather than giving the children poker chips, they were given tokens with bingo numbers stamped on them. At the beginning of the week, the parents would secretly pick a letter and number, and at the end of the week the child with the closest token to that number would be the one to receive dessert for dinner. The parents reported that the winning child often was willing to share the dessert with the other children, because the major excitement was in the program itself rather than being able to eat the dessert alone.

Some parents use random rewards in a much less formal method. One father, for example, simply announces at the beginning of a week that he has a particular treat in mind if everyone will do their jobs. Occasionally he will even specify what date the treat will be given so the children can avoid planning anything else for that time. Occasionally all the father says at the beginning of the week is, "If you work hard, I'll make it worth your while," and the children know from past experience that if they do a good job they will be rewarded with something worth having or doing. Sometimes the father simply announces that everyone should get in the car because they are going to get milkshakes; other times they will go on a family picnic together; and on one occasion the children didn't know until after they were out of town that they were headed on a four-day fishing trip four hundred miles away.

With all the merits and advantages of random reward programs, however, there is one disadvantage, and that is the anticipation of the event. The anticipation of an exciting experience is often greater than the experience itself. Random reward programs by their spontaneous nature fail to allow children to experience the joy of anticipation. Therefore, parents would be wise to adopt programs that contain both random rewards and predictable rewards.

## Summary

*Secondary rewards, especially social approval, are powerful reinforcers that motivate children.*

*Our behavior is more easily influenced by small, immediate, and definite reinforcers than it is by large, distant, and uncertain reinforcers.*

*Although our behavior is influenced by the environment, we still have the personal agency to decide what to do, and we can change our environment.*

*The three steps for properly rewarding good behavior are (a) describe the desired behavior, (b) explain why it was helpful, and (c) express appreciation.*

*Parents can successfully use a variety of reward programs to reinforce responsible behavior, such as allowances, points, gold stars, job charts, and random rewards.*

# 8

# Problem-Solving Skills for Parents

Jim knew that it was his responsibility to mow the lawn each week. He also knew that he needed to mow the lawn early because his Boy Scout troop was planning an overnight camp out this weekend. Before leaving for work Thursday morning, Jim's dad suggested that he mow the lawn that day. Jim ignored the suggestion, since he though he could mow it on Friday just as well. The troop didn't plan to leave town until 6:00 p.m Friday, and Jim assumed he would have plenty of time to get the lawn mowed. Before leaving for work Friday morning, Jim's dad again reminded him that he needed to mow the lawn, and emphasized the instruction by saying he would not be allowed to go camping with the Scouts until the lawn was mowed. "You won't be going anywhere until the lawn is mowed."

When Jim's father returned home from work at 5:30 p.m, he assessed the situation with one quick glance. Jim and three of his friends were on one side of the house playing basketball; four backpacks were propped against the front porch, ready to be taken camping; and the lawn mower was by the other side of the house with a few strips of cut grass. The father felt a sudden rush of anger as he realized that Jim had not completed the job he was assigned. "I should have been more firm last night. This is what I get for being so soft," he thought.

As he followed the sound of the bouncing ball, the irritation he felt inside grew more intense. Without waiting for play to stop he called to his son: "Jim, what were you supposed to do today?"

Jim glanced at his father before making a futile attempt to block his opponent's shot. "That's okay, Dad. You'll have to finish it yourself."

Failing to get the lawn mowed as instructed was bad enough, the father thought. Now he also had this defiant comment to reckon with. Jim's father decided that this situation called for a swift and firm response. "Who do you think you're talking to?" the father snapped. "Get over here." Jim was shocked to see his father's anger and immediately stared at him in surprise. Slowly he walked toward his father and wondered if there wasn't something he should say to his friends.

"Who do you think you're talking to?" the father repeated as Jim got nearer. "You know better than to talk to me that way." Jim tried to smooth the situation and struggled for something to say; nothing he said made any sense, however. "Go in the house," his father ordered. As Jim walked around the corner to go in the house, his father went over to his friends and asked for the basketball. "Why don't you take your packs and leave," the father suggested. "It doesn't look like Jim will be going with you. He hasn't done what I told him to do and he knows he was warned." The friends looked at each other, each hoping the other would say something. No one said anything, however, as they picked up their packs and walked away.

As he stood there holding the basketball, Jim's father considered forbidding Jim to play ball for the next week as punishment for failing to do his assigned job. He had already told him that he couldn't go camping if he didn't get the job done, and that apparently had not been sufficient punishment. Without resolving the debate in his mind, the father went in the house to talk to Jim.

"Why can't you be responsible?" the father began. "What do I have to do to make you realize that I'm serious?"

"You don't have to do anything," Jim said. He wanted to say more, but his father cut him off. As he waited for his father to finish so that he could explain the situation, Jim began to feel his own level of anger and resentment rising. "Why doesn't he just shut up and listen to me?" Jim thought as he listened to his father's harangue.

"What do you have to say for yourself?" the father finally asked. At last Jim had an opportunity to express his feelings and explain the situation, but by now it all seemed hopeless. His dad wasn't listening, nor did he want to understand. His friends had gone camping without him, and it was too late to get the job finished and join them on their camp out. In a tone of voice that sounded uncomfortably arrogant to the father, Jim simply replied, "Nothing."

This situation is characteristic of many of the problems parents face in raising children. On too many occasions small problems that should be easily handled become large problems as they are blown entirely out of proportion. If parents would learn how to solve problems correctly, however, the relationships between parents and children could be much happier. Jim's father could have resolved the problem better if he had used a different problem-solving approach. The correct approach consists of the following steps:

1. Describe the situation.
2. Diagnose whether it is an ability or motivation problem.
3. Use joint problem solving for ability problems.
4. Communicate consequences for motivation problems.
5. Handle emergent problems.
6. Decide who will do what by when and then follow up.[23]

As you learn each of these skills, take time to practice them. Don't just read them and think they are interesting, actually get a partner and practice using these skills.

## Describe the Situation

The first skill in learning how to solve problems is learning how to properly describe the situation. When you observe something wrong, your first response should be to describe the situation before taking action. The correct procedure for describing the situation is to—

- Be direct.
- Be specific.
- Be non-punishing.

The reason why you should be direct, specific, and non punishing can be illustrated by examining some of the incorrect methods parents typically use. For example, many parents respond to problems by pretending they are a grand inquisitor with an endless string of questions. Most of the questions don't make much sense, and they frequently don't deserve an answer. Jim's father, for example, could have asked, "Jim, what are you doing?" It doesn't take much of a sports fan to know that Jim was playing basketball. When children come home late they are frequently asked, "Can't you tell time?" or "Do you know what time it is?" They have been successfully telling time for several years; why should they forget now?

Getting angry and shouting at the child is also not a good way to respond to problems. This approach is often combined with various forms of name-calling and labeling, such as "You ornery brat" or "You rotten kid."

The opposite response is to ignore problems and pretend they don't exist. Many parents confuse ignoring problems with being patient. Certainly parents can't expect to discipline children for every trivial problem, but many parents ignore serious problems until the problems get too big or they can't stand it any longer. Then they realize that rather than ignoring the problem, they have been stockpiling their anger. At the top of their voice they finally begin to yell, "I've had it with you! I'm not going to stand this any longer!" or "That's it—you're really in for it now!"

Another approach used by some parents who attempt to be a bit more sophisticated is a smoothing approach, sometimes called sandwiching. Here parents begin and end by saying something sweet and nice, such as, "I know you want to be a good person" or "Usually you're such a good helper," but in the middle they torpedo the child with criticism and complaints. Parents think this sandwiching technique resolves the problem and leaves the child's self-esteem untouched. Most children feel, however, that they have been subjected to an ingratiating and insincere attack.

*Be direct*. In learning how to solve problems, you need to learn to be direct. When a problem exists, you need to discuss it openly and intentionally without beating around the bush. For example, suppose you were concerned that your daughter was not completing her homework. You could attempt to diagnose the problem using an indirect approach, which some parents confuse with being tactful. "What did you do after school this afternoon? How are you doing in school? How much TV have you watched already today? Did you spend your afternoon talking on the phone?" If you ask enough questions you may ultimately get the information you are after, but your daughter will probably feel like she is being set up or manipulated. If you want to know whether she has completed her homework, you ought to simply ask how much homework she was assigned and how much of it she has completed.

Suppose your son was expected to be home by midnight and he didn't return until 1:00 a.m. If you are concerned about him coming home an hour late—and you should—then you ought to discuss the problem directly. "Ken, you were supposed to be home by midnight, and you didn't make it until 1:00 a.m. What happened?" Some parents feel that if they are direct in approaching children about the problems, they will build a barrier between them and the child that will inhibit the flow of communication. Indeed, this is a legitimate fear, but if you begin asking Ken about the dance and who he danced with without talking first about the fact that he came home late, you are conveying either one of two messages: first, either the time he comes home isn't all that important, or, second, he's being buttered up with kindness before being bombed. If you are concerned about keeping channels of communication open, you can express how you feel but still be direct in handling the problem. "Ken, I'd like to have you tell me about the dance and who you danced with, but first we need to talk about the time you came home."

Learning how to be direct helps you to be less punishing. It is easier for children to talk to their parents about problems when the parents are direct. By discussing problems directly, there are no hidden agenda and no hidden motives. The atmosphere of the discussion is more open and honest. Problems can be resolved faster because both the parent and the child know where they stand and what the other person's feelings and motives are. A very simple phrase that helps parents learn to be direct is, "I'd like to talk with you about the problem of . . . ." This phrase helps parents convey to the child, simply and directly, the idea that there is a problem that needs to be solved.

*Be specific.* In describing problems, parents need to be specific in their description. Being specific teaches children what they did wrong and helps them avoid arguments with parents. The two elements of being specific include (1) stating a standard of acceptable performance and (2) describing the actual behavior. Both of these elements can be seen in the following statement: "Ken, you were supposed to be home by midnight and you didn't get home until 1:00 a.m." The advantages of being specific can be clearly illustrated by comparing specific and nonspecific descriptions. "Ken, you were late last night. Why are you always late?" "Ken, why can't you be more responsible? You're always so tardy." "Last night you were basically irresponsible." Most of the contentious arguments between parents and children result from parents failing to be specific as they describe problems. Ken is not always late and he would be quick to identify several recent occasions when he has been on time. The question, however, is not whether *always* means always or some of the time; the issue is that last night he was late.

As they describe the problem, parents should provide sufficient details so that the nature of the problem is accurately presented, but not so many details that the description becomes patronizing or punishing. For example, if a mother asked her daughter to clean the playroom and later found toys still scattered all over the floor, her description of the problem could be too specific: "The marble game is in the middle of the floor with fifty-six marbles scattered around it. The Goldilocks and the Three Bears card game is in one corner by the messy doll clothes. The blocks need to be picked up and stacked. The Legos are mixed with the checkers, and there are twenty-three little books scattered on the floor," and on and on. If the child didn't understand what constituted a clean playroom, all of this detail might be useful. However, this lengthy list of specific detail will generally appear overwhelming and a bit punishing.

*Be non-punishing.* When they are trying to describe the situation, parents should avoid being punishing in the description. If punishment or discipline is needed, it should occur later, after the problem has been adequately described and diagnosed. Parents have many ways of describing situations in a very punishing manner. Emotional outbursts and displays of anger are two obvious responses that are very punishing. But even if they don't get angry, and without screaming and shouting, parents can still be very punishing through a nasty tone of voice, condemning facial expressions, sarcasm, and other nonverbal behaviors. Using derogatory names or labels is a subtle form of punishment. "Well, slowpoke, you were supposed to have the table cleared twenty minutes ago." There are times when it is appropriate for you to show emotion, as will be described later. But a display of emotion, in the form of punishment, criticism, sarcasm, or anger, should not occur until after the problem has been diagnosed.

You need to look through the eyes of your child to detect whether your behavior is punishing or non-punishing. Many of the simple things parents do that are not intended to be punishing may nevertheless be perceived as punishment by the child. Pointing or shaking your finger at a child, holding your hands on your hips, staring intently at the child, standing above them, looking down, scowling, rolling your eyes, frowning, and other facial expressions can all be used to communicate disapproval and irritation.

## Diagnosing Problems: Ability Versus Motivation

After the situation has been described in a way that is direct, specific, and non-punishing, the parents need to diagnose the nature of the problem. The purpose of the diagnosis is to determine whether the problem is caused by a lack of ability or a lack of motivation. Parents need to respond much differently to problems that are caused by a lack of ability than to those caused by a lack of motivation. Therefore, after the problem has been described, parents should ask for a response from the child, "What happened?" "What went wrong?" "Am I right?" "Is there a reason for this that I don't understand?"

Knowing whether the problem was caused by a lack of ability or a lack of motivation is sometimes a very difficult decision. In some cases it is caused by both. A motivation problem is caused by a lack of motivation on the part of the child; the child could have done the job if he had wanted to and tried hard enough. An ability problem is caused by something beyond the control of the child; the child is too small, too young, inadequately trained, lacking knowledge, or lacking the proper materials and equipment.

Most problems are a combination of inadequate motivation and inadequate ability, and parents and children typically disagree about which is the most important. Parents generally think the problem was a lack of motivation. Children are more inclined to say they were willing, but the difficulty or inconvenience of the job prevented them from doing it. Some parents have the attitude that hard things take a little while to accomplish; the impossible only takes a little longer.

In the situation described earlier, the consequence would have been much different if Jim's father had carefully diagnosed the situation. "Jim, you were expected to mow the lawn before going camping today and the job isn't done. How come?"

"I mowed as much as I could until I ran out of gas. Remember I told you last week, Dad, when I emptied the can that we needed more gas, and you said you'd get some."

This situation is largely an ability problem. Jim was sufficiently motivated to do the job and mowed as much lawn as possible until the mower ran out of gas. It would have been possible for Jim to obtain money from his mother and ride his bicycle to a gas station to get some gas on his own. Although he couldn't carry a full three-gallon gas can home on his bike, he could have obtained enough gas to complete the job. Therefore, more motivation might have made a difference. However, Jim saw the problem strictly as an ability problem. He had told his father a week ago that he needed more gas, and his father failed to get it. He assumed that his dad would be home from work at five o'clock and that he could ask him to get some gas and still have plenty of time to get the lawn mowed before going camping. When his dad came home late, Jim assumed that it was now his father's problem and that there was nothing he could do until his dad made the next move.

Some situations appear to be such obvious motivation problems that it seems absurd to ask for an explanation of the problem after describing it. Swearing and teasing are good illustrations of such problems. When a child uses bad language or picks on a younger sibling, it seems silly for the parent to ask whether this behavior is a motivation or an ability problem. ("Do you know how to quit swearing?" or "Do you need to continue teasing?") Nevertheless, even when the behavior appears to stem from an obvious lack of motivation, the description of the problem could still conclude with a simple question asking the child to acknowledge the problem. "Is there any reason for this teasing that I don't understand?" or "Is there any good reason why you should continue to talk this way in the future?" Asking for a simple acknowledgment forces the child to objectively assess his or her behavior and think about its appropriateness. This type of objective self-assessment of their behavior helps to make children more responsive to analyzing their behavior and correcting it where it is wrong. Furthermore, parents are sometimes surprised to discover that what they assumed was a clear motivation problem was not as obvious as they thought. For example, the teasing that made them so upset may not have been teasing after all: "I wasn't teasing him; I only took his crayon away so he wouldn't write on the wall."

## Problem Solving for Ability Problems

When the problem is an ability problem, the appropriate response of the parents is to engage in joint problem solving with the child. Even when the problem is largely a motivation problem and only a small ability problem, it may still be useful for parents to engage in joint problem solving with the child. For example, suppose a child was asked to clip the grass around the trees. The parents view this request as a very simple instruction, and they see nothing preventing the child from completing this task. If the child wanted to do it badly enough, he could find the clippers and get the grass clipped. However, the child doesn't really want to do it all that badly. Having grass around the trees looks just fine to the child. Sure, he could get the job done if he really wanted to, even if he had to pull the grass away from the trees with his bare hands. Without looking, the child probably doesn't know where the clippers are hung in the garage and he may not really feel proficient in using them. So even though this situation is largely a motivation problem, part of the reason why it didn't get done is because it seemed to a young child that it was a difficult task to do.

In describing the situation, the parents may not get a clear enough statement from the child to indicate whether this is a motivation problem rather than an ability problem. In these situations it is useful for the parent to probe a little further to help clarify the situation for themselves and particularly for the child: "Are you saying you can't get the job done?" "I'm not sure I understand what the problem is yet." "It doesn't sound like you really want to do the job."

During a joint problem-solving session, both the parent and the child should participate in discussing the ways that the job can be accomplished. If the child does not know how to perform the job, he needs to be trained and will probably ask the parent to show how it can be done. If the child does not have the proper resources or materials, the parent will have to be responsible for providing them. At the conclusion of the joint problem-solving session, the parent and child should agree how to solve the problem and who does what by when.

Parents who interact effectively with their children in problem solving sessions are usually surprised to see how anxious their children are to prove their competence and ability. After you have determined how to solve the problem and who does what by when, you need to set a follow-up time when the task should be completed and then follow up as explained earlier.

## Communicating Consequences for Motivation Problems

Two different kinds of problems are classified as motivation problems: (1) when the child was capable of doing a task and knew that he was expected to do it and yet failed to accomplish it, and (2) when the child did something wrong and knew that it was wrong at the time he did it. In both of these situations the child could have behaved properly, but for some reason chose not to do so.

Imagine this: Four times within the last twenty minutes you have asked your son to take the garbage out, and each time he answered "Just a minute." Now you realize that he has gone out to play, and the sack of garbage is still sitting in the middle of the floor.

Or try this situation: Every day this week you have told the children not to shortcut across the patio because they then walk across the newly planted lawn on the other side. In spite of your warnings, however, there are clear footprints imbedded in the new lawn; so clear, in fact, that you can identify which child made each print.

These situations appear to be obvious motivation problems, and parents typically feel that they call for swift punishment. "Why can't they learn to be obedient?" "How many times do I have to tell them?" "What do I have to do to get them to change?" "I shouldn't have to tolerate this any longer." "I've had it up to here, and that's it." As you continue to talk to yourself and ask such questions, your feelings may go from a simmering irritation to a boiling anger. At times like these, parents need to stop stewing and start problem-solving. In fact, it would probably be better for your health and save your time to take the garbage out yourself and buy sod than to develop ulcers and high blood pressure or to fantasize punishments for your children.

So how should you handle the situation? First you need to talk with your child and describe the situation. "I asked you to take the garbage out. So why is it still sitting in the middle of the kitchen floor?" Chances are he forgot and all he needed was a brief reminder. It is unlikely that he faced an ability block, although there is an outside possibility that your spouse countermanded your instruction and sent him on another errand or some other unusual circumstance arose. By describing the situation in a way that is direct, specific, and non-punishing, you have at least allowed him the opportunity to say whether there were extenuating circumstances. Many motivation problems are essentially solved by describing the situation in a direct, specific, and non-punishing way. After the problem has been appropriately described, the child is willing to comply. Nevertheless, parents may still want to extend the learning from this situation to future situations. Before your son runs off to empty the garbage, therefore, you may want to make a few comments about the importance of obedience with a request that he obey more rapidly in the future and ask if there is any reason why he couldn't behave better in the future.

Serious motivation problems occur when the problem has been appropriately described and the child essentially responds with an attitude of "So what?" or "I don't want to." Now comes the real task of motivating behavior, and parents need to know the correct procedure for motivating children to perform. If a group of parents sat together in a brainstorming session and tried to list all of the possible ways of motivating stubborn children, they could probably identify hundreds of different techniques. This list would probably include a vast array of positive rewards, incentives, punishments, and threats. The one element all of these techniques would have in common is that they involve consequences of the child's actions. The consequences can be either positive consequences in the form of financial incentives, special privileges, and treats; or negative consequences in the form of spanking, verbal harangues, the denial of privileges, or the removal of rewards. All of these consequences have the potential of influencing behavior, but they are not all equally effective as long-term solutions to solving motivation problems.

In handling motivation problems there is a proper procedure for communicating consequences for a child's misbehavior. Following the proper order can contribute enormously toward solving motivation problems in a way that teaches positive values and helps to maintain a happy relationship between the parent and child. When parents follow the proper sequence of communicating consequences, children learn to be intrinsically motivated to behave properly. In the future, parents will not have to rely on their physical presence to monitor their children's behavior.

Motivation problems are solved by communicating consequences in this order:

1. Natural consequences
   a. to the task
   b. to others
   c. to you
2. Imposed consequences

Natural consequences refer to outcomes that occur naturally because of the demands of the situation. Imposed consequences, on the other hand, refer to consequences that bear no necessary relationship to the behavior of the child and are created by the parents or others. An example of a natural consequence is an infection created from an untreated cut. If a child scrapes her knee and does not clean it out, disinfect it, and cover it, it will almost certainly become infected. The parents didn't put the bacteria in the scrape, nor did they pass a rule that untreated cuts will become infected; the infection is a natural consequence of an untreated cut, and children must realize that if they don't take care of their scrapes they will become infected.

There are several natural consequences for failing to take the garbage out of the kitchen. First are the consequences to the task. If the garbage is not periodically taken out, it will continue to accumulate until a mountain of trash is stacked in the kitchen. Before long, the kitchen would smell as foul as a garbage dump. Second are the consequences to others. If the bag of garbage continues to sit in the middle of the floor, other family members will have to either take it out themselves or walk around it. It will likely get spilled and scattered all over the floor. In addition to the inconvenience to other family members, it will look unsightly and smell awful. Third are the consequences to you. The inconvenience to you, the parent, would be just as great as to any other family member if it is left in the middle of the kitchen, and since it can't remain there someone has to take it out. If you cannot get your child to do it, then you have to do it. But you shouldn't be expected to do everything without assistance from your children. You have other things you need to be doing with your time, and furthermore you expect your children to learn responsibility and to assume their share of family chores. Another part of the natural consequence to you is that if they don't behave as they should, you will feel very upset inside because of their irresponsible and uncooperative behavior. You expect them to do their fair share and contribute to the family responsibilities, and when they act irresponsibly you will naturally feel very upset and disappointed.

In communicating consequences, parents should communicate only as many consequences as are needed to obtain compliance. Natural consequences should be communicated at all three levels before imposed consequences are communicated. This order is just the reverse of what most parents are inclined to do. In fact, many parents are quick to communicate imposed consequences before they have even described the problem and diagnosed the possibility that it could have been caused by an ability block. Before imposing consequences, however, parents should carefully and systematically go through all three levels of the natural consequences. If the child willingly complies after the problem has been properly described, parents will not need to describe any consequences. Remember, the objective is to solve the problem and to get the job done, rather than to harass children or make them feel bad.

Second- and third-level natural consequences to others and to you should be communicated only if the child fails to respond to the natural consequences to the task. To illustrate, suppose you told your child, "We have told you not to walk across the new lawn, but I can see a lot of your footprints in the mud. Is there any good reason for this?" Hopefully this careful description will remind the child why he wasn't supposed to run across the new grass, and he will willingly comply and be more careful in the future. But suppose he says that he doesn't want to run all the way around the back of the patio because it takes too long and that he still plans to run across the new grass. The first consequence you should communicate is the consequence to the task: "If you keep running across the new grass, you will leave big footprints and kill the grass in those spots and it won't grow." This explanation will probably sound reasonable and he will be able to willingly comply. But suppose instead that he responds by saying, "So what difference does it make whether there's grass there or not?" Next, you should communicate the consequences to others: "If you continue to walk across the new lawn and kill it, everyone who walks around the house in the future after the sprinkling system has been on will get muddy feet, and the beaten path will not look very attractive." If he still has the same "Who cares?" attitude, you should communicate the third level of consequences: "I don't want to have an ugly yard with an unsightly footpath leading from the patio, and if you don't let the grass grow I'll have to lay sod, which is more expensive. I expect you to be obedient and adjust your playing to fit that. Running across the new grass isn't acceptable even during the most exciting moments of hide-and-seek."

After the natural consequences have proved to be ineffective, parents should then begin to use their list of imposed consequences. "If you walk across the new grass one more time, you will have to stay in the house and not be allowed to play with your friends outside." The appropriateness and effectiveness of various discipline techniques are described in chapter 9. In using imposed consequences, parents should remember two basic principles: parents should *be consistent* in administering the imposed consequences, and the consequences should *be fair.*

Although parents are inclined to use imposed consequences at the first sign of disobedience, they should appreciate the natural consequences associated with using natural consequences. In other words, using natural consequences as a discipline technique produces desirable outcomes. When parents use natural consequences, the child learns why the correct behavior is correct. Therefore, natural consequences are a useful mechanism for teaching. As a result of learning that natural consequences are associated with their behavior, children are able to acquire intrinsic rewards and personal values that change their behavior. Since natural consequences are not meant to be threatening to the child, a pleasant environment can be created and maintained between parent and child. Children are less likely to become rebellious and resistive when they realize that the consequences occur naturally and are not intended to injure or restrict them. An important advantage to parents in using natural consequences is that the natural outcome occurs without the parents having to be there to administer it. Parents do not have to wait by the grass and kill it every time the children walk across it. The new grass dies and leaves and ugly path without the parents having to do anything.

As parents communicate consequences to solve motivation problems, they need to remember to stop communicating consequences as soon as the person agrees to comply. If they continue to communicate consequences after compliance is achieved, the child will interpret this behavior as harassment and punishment. After the child agrees to comply, the final three steps in the problem-solving process are to decide who will do what by when, set a follow-up time, and then follow up. The delegation and follow-through processes were described in chapter 6.

If the child still refuses to obey after the parents have gone through the entire sequence of natural consequences, the parents then administer the imposed consequence: "If you can't play in the backyard without getting on the new grass, then you may not play in the backyard."

"Well, I won't promise."

"Okay, then, you can't play in the backyard; no swing set, no sandbox, no hide-and-seek."

A description of various natural and imposed consequences that parents can use, along with an assessment of their effectiveness, is provided in the following chapter.

The problem-solving process as it has been described so far has focused primarily on obtaining the child's agreement to behave obediently. The most difficult problems parents face, however, are not in getting children to consent but in getting them to actually obey. After they are told to do something, children typically agree to do it. But just because they agree to do it doesn't mean they follow through as they have been told. How should parents respond if children agree to do something and then fail to follow through?

If the child fails to follow through as agreed, this failure represents a new problem that should be handled with the same problem-solving procedure used with the first problem. The problem now, however, is the child's failure to follow through. "I need to talk to you about the new lawn again, son. Yesterday you said you would stay off of it and today I see new footprints. Didn't we have an agreement?"

As with the first problem-solving discussion, the parents' goal is once again to obtain compliance from the child to correct his or her behavior. This time, however, there are two simultaneous problems that have to be solved together—the original behavioral problem, and the failure to follow through as promised. Once again the parents should communicate consequences—natural consequences first and then imposed—until the child agrees to comply. Again, the purpose of the discussion is to obtain compliance rather than to harass, criticize, or condemn the child.

At this point you may be asking yourself, "What do I do if every time I go through the problem-solving discussion, the child agrees to comply before I ever state any imposed consequences and yet the child never follows through? How many times do I let them slip up before I take disciplinary action?" This question challenges parents to exercise their greatest judgment. If the children carelessly run across the grass time after time, at some point you're sure they deserve a spanking. But if they willingly comply and promise to do better each time you talk to them, and especially if they are sincere, there is probably something more than a lack of motivation involved here. They are probably running across the grass before they realize what they've done, and what they need more than a spanking is probably some form of barrier to prevent them from getting to the new grass.

## Dealing with Emergent Problems

Many times as parents are tying to describe the problem and diagnose whether it is an ability or motivation problem, the child will introduce a totally different issue. While you are trying to talk to your son about failing to take the garbage out, he begins to ask why his younger sister got to go to the movie yesterday and he didn't. These types of problems are referred to as emergent problems. They occur when a child feels he or she has a problem that is more important than the problem being discussed by the parents. Occasionally children may intentionally divert the parents by raising emergent problems—children are smarter than parents often realize. However, most children are sincere when they raise emergent problems, and in essence what they are saying is, "If you're going to clear the air and talk about something that's bothering you, then I want to have the air cleared for me, too, and talk about something that's bothering me." Although parents may feel frustrated by this diversion, they should remember that the child's problem is probably as important to the child as the parents' problem is to the parents.

When emergent problems arise, parents need to detour and deal with the emergent problem. "If my little sister got to go to the movie yesterday and I didn't, that's a serious miscarriage of justice. I'm being treated unfairly. Why does she get all the privileges and I don't get any? While she gets all the privileges, I have to do all the work around here. Let her take the garbage out; that's the least she can do. Maybe if I refuse to help out for a day or two, Mom and Dad will wise up and realize how important I am and know that they can't take me for granted any more."

When emergent problems arise, parents need to quickly assess how genuine and sincere the child's interest is in the emergent problem. Parents need to avoid being sidetracked by trivial issues that are not really important to the child. But if the emergent problem is indeed a serious problem, parents need to resolve the emergent problem before solving their own problem. Before proceeding to discuss the emergent problem, however, it is useful for parents to acknowledge that they are being sidetracked and indicate that they will return to their original problem once the emergent problem has been discussed. "Okay, son, let's talk about the movie, and then we'll talk about the garbage that's still sitting in the kitchen."

## Practicing Your Skills

Now that you have learned some new skills for solving problems, it is time to practice them. The following role-play episodes are designed for you to practice these skills with your spouse. The basic facts of each episode are only briefly described, and you may choose to embellish or alter this information as you desire. As you practice these skills, remember the following ideas: You don't need to pretend like you are someone you are not. These problem-solving skills represent a very simple and basic approach to handling parent-child interactions, and you can easily make them a part of your basic child-rearing skills.

For each episode there are two role descriptions, one role for the parent and the other for the child. Parents should alternate taking the role of the parent and child so that each has an opportunity to play both roles. After both of you have had an opportunity to read and study your roles, the parent should initiate the discussion by describing the situation. Before going on, you should then pause and discuss how the problem was described. Did the parent describe the situation in a direct, specific, and non-punishing way? Suggest a variety of ways for describing the situation before going to the next step. As the role play continues, the spouse who is playing the child's role must decide whether the problem is caused by a lack of ability, a lack of motivation, or both. You may want to go through each role play episode several times, once assuming the problem is an ability block and three or four times assuming the problem is caused by a lack of motivation and the child requires different levels of consequences before he is willing to comply. After compliance is achieved, the role play actors need to decide who does what by when and set a time for follow-up.

*Episode 1:  Piano Practicing*

*Parent:*  Your ten-year-old son is expected to practice the piano forty-five minutes per day. You don't expect him to play like Chopin, but since his lessons cost ten dollars a week you certainly expect to see him develop his skills. During the school year he was rather faithful in practicing, but the summer vacation seems to have destroyed the entire family's daily scheduling. His next lesson is in two days and you haven't heard him practice more than five minutes all week.

*Child:* You are expected to practice the piano forty-five minutes each day, but since it is summer vacation you like to goof off as well as any other ten-year-old. You didn't mind following your practicing schedule during the school year, but summer vacation isn't much of a vacation when you have to practice all the time. Besides, none of your friends do.

As the situation is described to you, listen to determine whether the description is direct, specific, and non-punishing. Discuss whether the description was punishing in tone. Try to decide what are some of the real reasons that discourage children from practicing and what kinds of consequences could change this situation.

*Episode 2: Washing Dishes*

*Parent:* Your family has a practice of taking turns doing dishes. The person who needs the most reminding about washing the dishes is your twelve-year-old daughter, who too often gets involved in some other activity and fails to wash the dishes. Last night it was her turn, but when you came home at ten o'clock you found that she had gone to bed without doing them. You did them for her. This morning you told her that she would have to take her turn tonight, but once again you walk in the kitchen at nine-thirty to find the table still covered with dirty dishes. Your daughter is downstairs watching television.

*Child:* Your family rotates the responsibility of washing dishes so that it is your job every sixth night. It's no fun washing dishes anyway, and especially bad when you have to come back to a kitchen full of dirty dishes. You are usually the first one through eating, and then leave to do something else while the others are finishing. Some members of the family eat so slowly that you can watch a full thirty-minute TV program before they finish. Last night you forgot to do the dishes and your parents had to do them for you. Tonight you were expected to do them and forgot again.

As the situation is described to you, determine whether it is described in a direct, specific, and non-punishing way. Before you respond, try to think of various reasons that would keep you as a twelve-year-old girl from doing the dishes, and what consequences could realistically get you to change your behavior.

*Episode 3: Feeding the Dog*

*Parent:* For years your son begged you to let him have a pet, so for his twelfth birthday you bought him a puppy and told him he was responsible to feed and train his dog. Everything worked out very well at first and it was fun to watch your son play with his puppy. After a few months, however, the novelty wore off and the dog did not get the attention it needed. The dog is not a puppy any more and has not been adequately trained. It has a bigger appetite and it makes bigger messes. Because of his forgetfulness, you feed the dog over half the time. Even worse, the dog has made the backyard a total mess. Yesterday the dog tipped over both garbage cans and garbage is scattered all over the yard.

*Child:* All your life you wanted a dog and your dreams came true when you turned twelve and received a puppy for your birthday. At first it was a lot of fun to play with your puppy, but as the dog got bigger a lot of the fun wore off. You didn't expect feeding and training a dog to take this much time and trouble. Last night your dog made a horrible mess because someone forgot to close the gate to the backyard. Since you didn't leave the gate open, you don't feel responsible for the mess.

As the situation is described to you, listen to determine whether the description is direct, specific, and non-punishing. You may want to wait until your parents communicate imposed consequences before you agree to comply, and even then your compliance may not be genuine.

*Episode 4: Hanging Up Wet Clothing*

*Parent:* When you go camping as a family, one of your basic rules is that everyone has to be responsible for hanging up their own wet clothing. Your eight-year-old, however, has difficulty remembering this rule. On several occasions already this week you have helped him by hanging up his clothing and informing him later about what you did. You just noticed that both his swimming suit and his sweater are lying in a pile, both soaking wet. You know he plans to use both articles of clothing tomorrow, and wonder if it wouldn't be better for you to say nothing and let him learn from his mistake. Putting on a cold, wet bathing suit before swimming in the lake is not too bad, but wearing a cold, wet sweater on an early-morning hike would be a long-remembered lesson.

*Child:* When you go camping with your family on family vacations, you are expected to hang up your own wet clothing. As an eight-year-old, you are not very good at remembering. You have forgotten to hang up your swimming suit and sweater, and you may have an unpleasant experience tomorrow because of your forgetfulness. To help you learn to be more responsible in the future, your parents may choose not to remind you.

After the situation is described to you, discuss the advantages and disadvantages of letting the child learn from his own mistake. What kinds of consequences should be communicated to eight-year-olds to help them avoid this type of problem in the future?

*Episode 5: Teasing*

*Parent:* There is nothing that causes greater contention in your family than the constant teasing between your ten-year-old son and your nine-year-old daughter. In the past year the relationship between them has deteriorated to the point of open warfare. They are constantly criticizing each other and saying unkind words. The relationship is so toxic, in fact, that if one smiled at the other, there would come the accusation, "He pulled a face at me." You have just rushed to the kitchen to arbitrate a civil war. This most recent battle started with a shouting match over who held rights to the possession of a chair in front of the TV. The verbal battle quickly escalated to full-scale war. As you enter the kitchen, there is a broken dish on the floor, chairs tipped over, and the son has the daughter's arm pinned against the wall while she is kicking his shins. She has blood dripping from her nose because she bumped it against his head. He has blood oozing from a scratch on his forearm.

*Child:* In your family there is an eight-year-old daughter and a ten-year-old son. You are one of them and can't stand the other. Your sibling (brother or sister) makes fun of everything you do and is constantly teasing you. In the past you have been rather patient, but now you've taken all you're going to take. This afternoon you were sitting in a chair in front of the TV and got up to go to the bathroom. Before you left the chair, you clearly said "Saved," but when you came back, guess who was in it and refused to get out? Any more it seems like the only thing that counts around here is physical force, and if that's what it takes, that's what you're willing to give.

As the situation is described to you, observe whether it is direct, specific, and non-punishing. Before you begin to respond, think carefully about the kind of consequences that it will take to achieve compliance. Are there any consequences, even the most severe imposed consequences, that could get you to willingly and genuinely comply, unless your sibling agrees to comply first?

*Episode 6: Coming Home Late*

*Parent:* When your daughter turned sixteen and you talked with her about dating, she agreed with the family rule that except for special occasions, she would be home by midnight. Friday night, however, she failed to come in until 12:30, and Saturday night she failed to come in until almost 1:00 a.m.

*Child:* The rule in your family is that when you go out at night you are required to return by midnight. Friday night you went on a date and spent so much time talking with your friends at a pizza parlor that you didn't get home until 12:30 a.m. Saturday night you went on a date to a one-act play contest where you were one of the participants. The plays lasted much longer than you anticipated, and by the time the winning plays were announced, the sets were dismantled, and everything was cleaned up, even the cast party had to be cut short. You still didn't get home until 1:00 a.m. Obviously you think that the things you were doing were more important than a few minutes of sleep.

As the situation is described to you, analyze whether it was direct, specific, and non-punishing. Listen carefully to the natural consequences that are described for staying out late. Try to generate a list of the natural consequences that you think are really significant.

## Summary

*The correct problem-solving approach for parents consists of five steps:*

1. *Describe the situation in a way that is direct, specific, and non-punishing.*
2. *Diagnose whether the problem was caused by a lack of ability or a lack of motivation.*
3. *If the problem was caused by a lack of ability, use joint problem solving to generate a solution.*
4. *If the problem was caused by a lack of motivation, get the person to agree to improve by communicating consequences in this order:*
   a. *Natural consequences—*
      *(1) to the task or situation;*
      *(2) to others;*
      *(3) to you.*
   b. *Imposed consequences.*
5. *Handle emergent problems.*
6. *Decide who will do what by when and then follow up.*

# 9

# Discipline
# Techniques

Disciplinary problems should be viewed as behavior problems, not as personality problems. Parents should avoid playing amateur psychologists and not look for underlying personality problems in their child's disobedience. If a child forgets to make his bed, you need to realize that this may be just a simple act of forgetfulness rather than a character flaw of laziness or personal irresponsibility. While it is true that children are developing basic behavioral patterns, it is far better for you to focus on correcting your children's behavior rather than trying to change their personalities. Behavior is easier to change than personality. In fact, the easiest way to change your child's personality, if you should decide to do so, is to get the child to change his behavior.

The problem-solving process described in chapter 8 explained how you should handle misbehavior problems. If the problem is caused by a lack of ability, you should engage the child in a joint problem-solving discussion. But if the problem is caused by a lack of motivation, you should communicate conse-

quences to the child: first, natural consequences to the task, to others, and to you; and then imposed consequences. This chapter examines the kinds of consequences you can use to solve behavioral problems. Parents use a variety of disciplinary methods that can generally be categorized as
1. natural or logical consequences;
2. psychological punishment;
3. spanking and power-assertive techniques;
4. induction and modeling.

## Natural or Logical Consequences

After reminding your thirteen-year-old son for several days to clean his room, you finally decide to go upstairs and inspect the situation. The room is such an atrocious mess it can hardly be called a bedroom. Clothes, books, papers, and model airplane parts are scattered all over. The mattress doesn't even have sheets on it, and the bed probably has not been made for weeks. And yet every time you asked your son if his room was clean, he said it was okay. When he was younger, you were willing to help him clean his room, but now you expect him to assume the responsibility for cleaning it himself. Obviously, he is not doing a very good job.

When children misbehave, a variety of consequences may follow their behavior. These consequences can generally be divided into one of three categories: imposed consequences, natural consequences, or logical consequences.

*Imposed consequences* are sometimes called contrived consequences because they are created by parents and administered arbitrarily. Imposed consequences include both punishments and rewards. Punishment includes such things as spanking children, "time-outs" by themselves, sitting them on a chair, refusing to let them have desserts, forbidding them to leave the house, and prohibiting them from watching television. Rewards include such incentives as giving them an extra dollar per week allowance or an opportunity to go to the movies if they do their job. These punishments and rewards have no logical relationship to the messy room; they are arbitrarily imposed by parents to reward good behavior or punish misbehavior. An example of some imposed consequences associated with the dirty room include, "You don't get to go to the movies if your room is a mess," or "You're not allowed to ride your bicycle unless you clean your room." These consequences are quite unrelated to having a dirty room.

*Natural consequences* refer to the results of the child's behavior that occur because of the laws of nature or society. For example, if your son throws his wet bathing suit wrapped in a towel on the bottom of his closet floor and leaves it there for three days, it will be wrinkled and covered with mildew. No one had to spread mildew all over it or spray it with an unpleasant odor. These consequences occurred naturally. Likewise, if you're too lazy to gather firewood and build a fire, the natural consequence is that you stay cold.

Natural consequences are associated with all forms of misbehavior, and they are generally superior to imposed consequences. The natural consequence of a messy room, for example, is that your son's clothes will not look nice, and his model airplane parts are likely to get lost, broken, or damaged. Some natural consequences are virtually certain to occur, others are highly probable, and some are not very probable, but there is at least a possibility. For example, it is certain that the messy room will look unsightly and the dirty clothes will not be properly laundered and ready to wear. The probability that the model airplane parts will get broken and lost is very high. It is not certain that he will lose something important like his wallet or his Eagle Scout application, but with such a messy room many important things are likely to get lost.

Sometimes parents complain that they have difficulty identifying the natural consequences for a particular act:

"When my children are bickering back and forth, I don't care what the natural consequences are, I just want to spank them."

"Regardless of the natural consequences, I want my daughter home by midnight. If she's not home by then, she's grounded."

"I can't explain why swearing or sassing me is wrong, but I'll send them to their room if they ever do it."

"Whether I can think of any good reasons or not, he's got to have his hair cut."

What these parents are saying is that they feel very strongly that certain behaviors are inappropriate even if they cannot explain the natural consequences justifying them. A useful rule of thumb for parents to remember is that if they cannot identify meaningful, natural consequences, they ought to question whether the bad behavior is really bad. Doing something "because I said to" or "because it's the rule" is not a very legitimate explanation. Parents and children need rules, and it is legitimate for parents to enforce family rules. However, parents ought to be able to identify natural consequences justifying the rules. If you concentrated for a few minutes, you could identify several natural consequences of swearing, staying out late, disrespectful behavior, bickering, and unsightly long hair. All you need is one good natural consequence to justify a rule.

There are natural consequences associated with using natural consequences. In other words, when parents use natural consequences, they obtain desirable results that are superior to imposing their own consequences. The natural consequences of using natural consequences are—

- The person learns why the correct behavior is correct.
- Since natural consequences are not threatening, a pleasant environment is created between parent and child.
- The child is less likely to become rebellious and resistive.
- Natural consequences will remain even when the parents are not around.
- Intrinsic rewards and personal values, such as responsibility and initiative, are acquired by the child.

Although natural consequences are associated with all forms

of misbehavior, they are frequently so far removed in time and place from the event that they are not useful learning experiences. For example, the consequences of teasing or being unkind to a friend usually come several months later when the child is not invited to a party or is the last one selected when choosing sides to play baseball. Therefore, parents frequently need to intervene and structure more visible and immediate logical consequences. The consequences should be logically related to the misbehavior and occur as soon as possible after the misbehavior.

*Logical consequences* are a form of imposed consequence in the sense that they are contrived by the parents. However, logical consequences contain a logical relationship to the violated rule. For example, when your son refuses to keep his room clean, a logical consequence would be to not allow him to invite any of his friends over to his house until his room is clean. It is logical for parents to not want others to see a messy house, and his messy room is a major factor contributing to a messy house. "If you don't keep your bedroom clean, your friends cannot come here to play. We don't want them seeing a messy house, and they will only add to the mess you refuse to clean."

Although natural and logical consequences are superior to imposed consequences, there are times when imposed consequences are appropriate. When children fail to comply after parents have communicated the natural consequences, the parents should appropriately administer the imposed consequence. One way to make imposed consequences more effective is to involve children in constructing and developing the consequence. "If anyone forgets to do the dishes when it is his turn, what should be the punishment?" If children participate in making the rules, they are more inclined to obey them and accept the consequences when they disobey. Small children are obviously not prepared to participate very effectively in designing imposed consequences. But as they mature and become more personally responsible, they should become more involved in the design of the rules they must follow and the consequences they must suffer for misbehavior. When children participate in setting the rules, parents have an opportunity to explain the justifications for the rules and to teach moral principles.

## Psychological Punishment

Psychological punishment refers to shaming the child, appealing to his pride, ridiculing him, rejecting him, and other forms of inducing guilt. This kind of punishment can appear in several forms: for example, the parent—

Explicitly withholds love:

"I don't like you when you talk like that."

"All right, don't ask me to help you anymore."

Threatens to withhold love:

"If you keep that up I'll go downstairs and leave you alone."

"You won't get your good-night kiss if you keep on whining."

Expresses strong disapproval of the child or his actions:

"You ought to be ashamed of yourself for hitting someone smaller than you."

"Nice children don't do that."

"That was a very bad thing to do."

"You rotten kid! I can't stand you."

Psychological punishment also includes shouting, yelling, screaming, and other forms of scolding. To the extent that the scolding contains some form of reasoning or explanation for why the behavior is wrong, this type of discipline would be classified as induction. However, scoldings that simply vent the parents' anger and frustration are considered psychological punishment.

There has been some speculation that psychological punishment contributes to moral development through the process of identification. Withholding love from a child when he misbehaves can arouse anxiety within the child over losing the parents' love. To reduce this anxiety the child supposedly tries to identify with his parents and learns to control his impulses by adopting their thoughts, feelings, and behaviors. However, this speculation is not supported.[24]

The benefits of psychological punishment and withholding love from children are questionable, and parents should not rely on them to teach moral values to their children. When the family atmosphere is generally affectionate, psychological punishment can arouse guilt—but it does not create desirable moral behavior. Studies on the effects of specific love-withdrawal techniques have shown that strong psychological punishment can result in excessive anxiety and inhibition, which sometimes leads to extreme mental disturbances. Psychological punishment has been found to result in a lack of generosity in children, reduced resistance to temptation, increased cheating, and more aggressive behavior.[25]

The only time that love withdrawal appears to contribute positively to moral development is when it is accompanied by reasoning, explanation, and other teaching procedures, because love withdrawal makes the child more susceptible to adult influence. As a general rule, rejection, ridicule, and withholding love, make children feel remorseful about their misbehavior, but it does not teach or reinforce good behaviors.[26]

## Spanking and Power-Assertive Techniques

Power-assertive techniques include all forms of physical punishment, including spanking, whipping, slapping, and beating. It also includes other techniques whereby parents impose their demands on the child through direct commands, threats, deprivation, or physical force with no explanation and no attempt to compensate the child for being forced against his will. Some power-assertive techniques can be fairly neutral, such as reaching over to turn off a child's radio when it is too loud. Other power-assertive techniques are much more violent, such as slapping a child across the mouth for speaking out of turn. The use of power-assertive techniques in either fashion tell the child that despite his wishes of the moment, he must without question stop what he is doing and comply immediately.

In using power-assertive techniques the parents impose their personal will arbitrarily rather than make a legitimate demand. If the demand was required by some physical or social reality rather than by the arbitrary exercise of parental authority or physical force, it would be considered a legitimate demand. An example of a legitimate demand would be making a child move a pile of stacked blocks to permit the repairman to remove an appliance. However, ordering a child to put down a noisy toy just so the parents can hear the television would be an example of power-assertion. Here, there is no physical or social reality requiring the child to cease playing with the toy. Taking the noisy toy away from the child may help the parents maintain their sanity, but it was necessary only because the parents arbitrarily decided it was necessary.

The use of intense physical punishment as a means of altering behavior has been frequently and repeatedly condemned. For example, a series of studies involving six-to eight-year-old children indicated that punishment not only failed to communicate to the children the appropriate response, but it was also not especially effective in helping them avoid undesirable behaviors. To suppress undesired behavior through punishment, parents are required to use the right combination of four variables: the timing of the punishment, the intensity of the punishment, consistency, and an affectionate relationship. In order for parents to effectively suppress undesired behavior by punishing it, the punishment should occur almost immediately after the undesired behavior, and the punishment must be mildly and consistently applied after every undesired act. Furthermore, for punishment to be effective, the parent and child need an affectionate relationship. Because punishment tends to destroy such a relationship, parents must spend considerable time creating an affectionate relationship at other opportunities to offset the effects of punishment. In short, parents should not rely solely on punishment to suppress unacceptable forms of behavior and teach their child proper social behavior. Punishment can only be effective when judiciously used and combined with other forms of discipline.

Studies on the effects of child-rearing practices have consistently shown that power-assertive techniques are generally inconsistent with moral development. As a general rule, arbitrary discipline and harsh punishment create delinquency and aggressive behavior. Two studies of aggressiveness, for example, one examining a lower-class population and the other a middle-class population, both produced similar conclusions. The aggressive, antisocial children emerged from an environment characterized by parental rejection, family discord, punitive discipline, and inconsistent punishment.[27]

An excellent longitudinal study of family variables associated with aggression also found aggressiveness related to power-assertive discipline techniques. This study examined 174 boys who were first evaluated between 1939 and 1945, and reevaluated later in 1956. Using information that was obtained from various sources, some boys were classified as aggressive and others were classified as nonaggressive. The aggressive boys were more frequently disciplined in a punishing way by their parents, more frequently threatened, and more likely to have been rejected by their parents. The nonaggressive boys generally came from families that placed high demands on them for polite and responsible behavior, and they were more likely to have been closely supervised, but seldom were they physically threatened or punished.[28]

In summary, power-assertive techniques are appropriate in only a limited number of situations. They may be necessary for young children who do not understand rational explanations, and they might be necessary when there are time constraints or safety considerations preventing parents from explaining their demands. When children are guilty of willful disobedience, a good, sound spanking is also appropriate, as will be discussed later. But the overwhelming weight of evidence indicates that power-assertive techniques are generally inappropriate. They not only fail to teach moral behaviors, they are incompatible with moral development when they are used excessively. Furthermore, they don't contribute to the happy family relationships that ought to characterize the home environment.

# Induction and Modeling

Induction and modeling were introduced earlier in chapter 4 to explain how values become internalized. These two processes are also two of the best discipline techniques. Induction includes all forms of verbal explanations, such as teaching, preaching, reasoning, and explaining. Induction provides knowledge and information describing appropriate behaviors and a justification for why those behaviors are appropriate. The results of many studies indicate that induction is a useful if not necessary technique in moral development. Parents who use induction to explain the implications of their children's behavior on others generally have children who show more consideration for others, are more resistant to temptations, and are less aggressive. Laboratory studies have demonstrated that induction techniques tend to increase altruistic behaviors.[29]

One writer has suggested that induction leads to moral internalization primarily because of the parent-child interaction during a discipline encounter.[30] According to this explanation, the discipline encounter is the major interaction where moral behaviors are acquired. In the encounter, the desires of the child and the moral demands of the parents have to be resolved. The child is compelled in this encounter to achieve a balance between expressing his desires and controlling them. For example, if your son takes a candy bar from a store and you catch him eating the stolen merchandise, you need to take some kind of disciplinary action. How you handle this situation will influence your son's moral values—whether you spank him, verbally scold him, make him return the uneaten portion, make him pay for it, or explain why shoplifting is wrong.

The difference between power-assertive techniques and induction during the discipline encounter is very dramatic. Power-assertive techniques compel the child to compare his desires against the parents' anticipated punishment. This perception creates a feeling of opposition between parent and child and reinforces the idea that the sources of moral standards are external to the child. (If I get caught stealing a candy bar, I will be punished.) However, the effects of induction are to direct the child's attention to the natural consequences of his behavior and the logical demands of the situation. (Taking a candy bar is wrong because it is stealing. People who steal can be put in jail, and the stores would go out of business if everyone stole from them.) Thus, with induction, rather than thinking about the punitive consequences to himself, the child is thinking about the consequences of his behavior on other individuals. As a result, induction techniques provide the child with an intellectual understanding of the consequences of his actions and allow him sufficient freedom to think about this information for himself. The individual thereby controls his own behavior and forms an internal basis for his moral standards.

Modeling refers to the example parents set for their children to follow; it also has a powerful influence on the development of moral behaviors. Abundant evidence shows that modeling is an extremely effective technique in developing moral values. Modeling processes have been studied at great length, and studies have shown that modeling influences the amount, direction, and durability of moral behaviors, especially altruism. Furthermore, there is increasing evidence showing that vicarious learning from observing a model can effectively change an individual's behavior.[31]

Modeling helps children develop positive moral values in many ways. Observing a model serves as a form of new information and knowledge for the child, especially in novel situations. If a child never had to decide how to behave in a new situation, then the example of a model not only teaches the child the best way to behave but also tells the child that this is the most appropriate way. Five-year-olds, for example, have never been five before, and they are not sure how a five-year-old should respond to new situations. By observing their parents or other five-year-olds, however, they learn different ways to behave, and the fact that someone else behaves a certain way is a signal that it's probably okay for them to behave that way also.

The effects of modeling on moral development increase as the model becomes more attractive. Behaving like a model becomes increasingly reinforcing as the model becomes increasingly attractive. Considerable research evidence has shown that the attractiveness of a model has a significant influence on the development of modeled behavior. Aggressive boys, for example, tended to have fathers who displayed aggressiveness in their own behavior, while nonaggressive boys tended to have fathers who provided a parental model of responsibility and control over their deviant impulses.[32] Individuals who are not respected or held in high esteem are generally not modeled. Many of the aggressive boys did not have an influential father influencing their behavior. Consequently, many of the aggressive boys were influenced relatively less by their fathers and relatively more by factors outside the home, especially neighborhood groups. Another study of child-rearing practices among the fathers of delinquent adolescents versus normal adolescents found that a far greater number of delinquents perceived their fathers as ineffective, negative, and emotionally unstable.[33]

## When Should Parents Show Emotion?

The research evidence clearly shows that the calm and rational techniques of induction and modeling are far more effective than psychological punishment or power assertive techniques in teaching moral values. Does this mean that parents should never get angry? Should parents ever show emotion? Should they try to develop such total control over their feelings and emotions that all forms of discipline are administered in a calm, rational, and unruffled manner?

It is not wrong for you to show emotion. In fact, you need to show emotion and develop congruence with your feelings. However, your feelings should not be anger and hatred toward your child. Instead, the feelings that you ought to express should be disappointment and grief because of the child's behavior. You should never strike a child or physically shake him in the heat of emotion when you have lost your temper and you are out of control. Many disastrous cases of child abuse, some even resulting in death, have occurred when parents were trying to discipline children in the heat of emotion. Shocked and remorseful parents say they didn't mean to hit or shake them that hard, but little bones and bodies have become severely damaged when disciplined in the heat of anger.

One mother's most priceless heirloom was a vase that her great-grandmother had brought from her homeland. The vase was very carefully stored on a high shelf out of reach of young children. Unfortunately, it was not out of reach of a baseball, and the mother watched horrified as the baseball struck the vase and saw it plummet to the floor. The shattered glass was beyond repair and so were her feelings. How many times had she told them not to throw balls in the house? For just a moment she thought of getting the yardstick and beating both boys until the yardstick was reduced to toothpicks. Instead, she went quickly to her bedroom, locked the door, and cried. Not until she was once again calm and composed did she emerge from the bedroom to see that the boys had cleaned the glass. No punishment, she concluded, would bring back the vase, and any display of emotion on her part she thought would only be a sign of personal weakness. Unfortunately, this mother failed to use this opportunity to teach her children a valuable lesson. By hiding her emotions she deprived her sons of the opportunity to learn from their mistake.

The father of three grade school children walked into the family room of their new home and discovered that the children had taken coals out of the fireplace and rubbed charcoal across the grouting of the new brick fireplace. The father, who was normally a very calm individual and not prone to show much emotion, paused briefly to decide how this situation should be handled. A spanking did not seem appropriate because there was no evidence of willful disobedience, but simply stopping the children and handling the problem in a calm, unemotional manner appeared to overlook an excellent teaching moment. After a few seconds he decided what to do and formulated the monologue in his mind.

"Oh, no," he began. "Look at our new fireplace! It's got charcoal all over it! Oh, how awful! Now it's going to look ugly! Oh, no! This is just awful!"

As he continued his monologue describing how unsightly and deplorable the fireplace looked and how their new home was being carelessly destroyed, the father fell to his knees, beat his hands on the floor, swung his arms dramatically in the air, and buried his face in his hands. Although the children were never threatened or specifically punished, they were greatly touched by their father's display of overwhelming grief and emotion. Without realizing that the father's grief was being substantially overdramatized, the children quickly obtained water and rags and attempted to clean the fireplace. This father maintained that his emotional display on this occasion contributed significantly over the following years to help his children appreciate the value of their new home and the importance of taking good care of it.

When disciplining children, it is appropriate for you to display your emotions when your emotions are mature adult emotions. It is not right for you to lose your temper and to physically or psychologically assault your child. But when you feel intense disappointment and unhappiness, you ought to make your feelings known. Expressing your feelings helps your children to understand your values. You value most the things that create feelings of emotion—happiness, disappointment, or anxiety—and it would seem awkward and unnatural to discipline your children in a cold, calm, and unfeeling manner.

## Handling Disobedience

When children disobey, parents want to know how they should handle the disobedience. "When my child is ornery and complaining, when I catch my children fighting, or if they refuse to do the job I have asked them to do, how should I handle these problems?" It would be nice if child care were as simple as lawn care—you water it when it's dry, mow it when it's tall, and fertilize it when it's hungry. Unfortunately, raising children is far more complex than caring for a lawn. Human nature is very complex, and the appropriate type of parental discipline is not always the same. Parents need to alter the discipline to fit the cause of the disobedience. Different forms of disobedience require different kinds of discipline. Some of the major causes of disobedience and the appropriate discipline for each include the following.

**Physical discomfort.** The first cause of misbehavior is physical discomfort. When babies are uncomfortable, they cry. When children are hungry or tired, they become irritable and disagreeable and tend to whine and complain. When they are ill or in pain, they act ornery and do not behave as they might otherwise be expected to behave. When teenagers stay out late night after night and fail to get enough sleep, they tend to feel tired and lazy. Many teenagers would be much less defiant and rebellious when things don't go their way if they weren't so tired.

If a child's misbehavior is caused by physical discomfort, parents should try to remove the discomfort while showing sympathy and understanding. At one time it was recommended that babies be fed on a fixed schedule regardless of when they became hungry. Medical advice now suggests that infants should be fed when they are hungry while gradually moving them toward a regular schedule. In general, the same advice holds for other forms of physical discomfort. Parents need to patiently satisfy their children's physical needs while encouraging them to control their irritability and whining.

Unfortunately, parents cannot eliminate all pain and discomfort. Children need to learn socially acceptable ways of behaving even when they are tired, hungry, or ill. Simply experiencing pain, however, will not by itself do much to help children respond well to discomfort. What they need is a compassionate model and patient explanations to accompany their pain. "I know you're hungry but please try to be patient." "I'm sorry it hurts, but there isn't anything we can do. Try not to think about it." "Yes, it's a long time to sit still, but you can do it—just make up your mind to do it." Parents will most likely find that their explanations and reasoning will be much more effective after the discomfort is reduced. It's easier to learn that there is dignity associated with silently enduring necessary pain when you can think calmly and rationally about it rather than when you're enduring intense pain.

**Curiosity.** The second cause of misbehavior is curiosity. There are objects that arouse curiosity for children of every age. For infants the object could be almost anything they can put in their mouth. For two-year-olds it could be a flower vase, a precious necklace, or a set of marking pens that leave bright colored marks on the wall. For eight-year-olds it could be a father's desk computer. For twelve-year-olds it could be a motorcycle or their own anatomy. For fifteen-year-olds it could be a car or another person's anatomy.

The customary advice to parents here is to remove the object from the environment and eliminate the curiosity. For young children this is good advice, since the only discipline technique that has any chance of suppressing the curiosity is mild consistent physical punishment. Most parents, however, do not have the time or interest required to combine the correct timing, degree of punishment, consistency, and affection that are needed to effectively punish each undesired response.

As children mature, however, they gradually develop the thinking skills (called cognitive structures) needed to control their curiosity, and you need to explain why they must control their curiosity. Induction techniques help children develop internal control of their own behavior. You can also help satisfy or minimize the curiosity by showing how the desk calculator functions and by taking the child for a motorcycle ride. Another useful strategy is distraction when the curiosity can't be satisfied. An expensive necklace could be  replaced by a toy. Interest in a car or the opposite sex can be redirected into other interesting and personally enriching things such as hobbies, skills, talents, and athletics.

**Carelessness.** The third cause of misbehavior is carelessness. In the life of a child, countless unpleasant incidents occur because of carelessness: milk gets spilled, dishes get dropped, lamps get knocked over, and windows get broken. These are accidents that would not have happened if the child had been more careful. In most instances, the child is guilty of a mis-appraisal of the situation. Usually the child knows he should have acted differently, and if he had followed his parents' instructions the unnecessary event would not have occurred. In some instances, however, the cause of the accident is beyond the child's accountability. When he rushed in the back door, for example, he had no way of knowing he would spill a can of paint. Like all accidents, it might have been prevented, but the child could not have been expected to foresee the result.

The frustrated and angry feelings of parents are usually the same regardless of whether the incident resulted from carelessness or an innocent accident. Unfortunately, parents sometimes lack the maturity to adequately control their feelings, and they respond to the severity of the accident rather than the cause of the accident. If the incident resulted from an unfortunate accident or if the child could not have been expected to anticipate the accident, there is no reason for punishing the child either physically or psychologically. However, natural consequences might be used effectively by having the child clean up the mess. Induction techniques might also be useful in explaining the cause of the accident, thereby reducing the likelihood of a repeated occurrence.

When the accident results from carelessness, especially if the child has just been warned, parents tend to over-respond with some form of physical or psychological punishment. Yelling and spanking, however, are not as helpful as a patient explanation of the need to be more careful. Furthermore, the effects of severe punishment usually contribute not to future carefulness but to future secretiveness—nobody is responsible for the broken dish on the floor; it must have fallen on the floor by itself. Such lies may be wrong, but they are rational to the child.

**Forgetfulness.** The fourth cause of misbehavior in children is forgetfulness—forgetting to make their beds, forgetting to brush their teeth, forgetting to wipe their feet, forgetting to practice the piano, forgetting to bring home their lunch boxes, forgetting to do their homework. As the child matures, his capacity for remembering gradually increases. When his intellectual functioning is sufficiently complex, he can remember complex instructions and show responsibility and initiative. The intellectual development of children proceeds at different rates. Parents should patiently wait until their child has developed adequate cognitive structures before they can expect him to remember very much.

An especially difficult concept for children to grasp is a sense of time. Even children in grade school after they have learned to tell time usually have extreme difficulty judging when thirty minutes have passed. Therefore, telling a child to come home in thirty minutes is a formidable instruction. No discipline technique will be as useful here as a reminder from someone that thirty minutes have passed.

Parents are frequently irritated with preschool children when they play with several toys and forget to put them away. In spite of their irritation, however, parents need to realize that the mental association between "I'm through playing" and "Now I need to put away my toys" is extremely unnatural and unlikely. One reason why the first concept will not trigger the second concept is that children seldom decide they are through playing. They just proceed to the next activity. This does not mean the two concepts cannot be associated or that children should never have to pick up their toys, but it means that one or two explanations will not be adequate, especially with young children. Toddlers may need to be reminded to pick up their toys every time. Forgetfulness can even be expected in teenage years. At every age there are age-related causes of forgetfulness, such as exciting new experiences like learning to roller skate, learning to play basketball, or learning to talk on the phone when you don't have anything to say.

If the reason for forgetfulness is a lack of intellectual development, neither physical or psychological punishment will solve the problem. Punishment will only produce negative results, such as guilt, anxiety, fear, and hatred toward the parents. But when parents are convinced that the child has adequate mental ability to remember and still forgets, the most useful technique is a well-designed system of natural and logical consequences. If you forget to come home on time for dinner, you have to eat cold, dried food. If you forget to brush your teeth, you don't get to have desserts tomorrow. If you forget to practice the piano today, you don't get to play outside tomorrow. Mild forms of physical or psychological punishment can also help decrease forgetfulness if they are combined with rational explanations and reasoning. Many parents have effectively used gold stars, money, allowance, points, and other systems that reward children for remembering, or deprive them of rewards if they forget. These systems are intended not only to reward good behavior but also to help children remember. The goal is to have children monitor their own behavior and develop responsibility and initiative.

**Objectionable mannerisms.** The fifth cause of misbehavior is bad habits and objectionable mannerisms, such as squirming, nose picking, mouth noises (sucking air between the teeth or grinding the teeth), tics (muscle twitches and facial grimaces), and obnoxious social mannerisms designed to get attention. According to psychoanalysis, some of these objectionable mannerisms are outward expressions of internal disturbances. Trying to eliminate one tic without resolving the internal stress would only add to the problem and result in another tic appearing that may be even more objectionable. Psychoanalytic counseling with a trained analyst is occasionally required to resolve the internal stress or disturbance. However, most objectionable mannerisms can be eliminated with patient encouragement.

Parents can help enormously even when professional help is needed by providing a supportive climate in which the child receives abundant attention and concern. If the child is misbehaving to get attention, parents need to eliminate the need for the inappropriate behavior by ignoring it as much as possible and compensating for their lack of concern by showing a lot of attention and interest at other times.

The principle of *extinction* should be used by parents to its greatest extent in eliminating undesirable mannerisms. Extinction refers to the removal of positive reinforcement and often takes the form of ignoring the act. Parents should try to eliminate all forms of positive reinforcement for these behaviors. Some objectionable mannerisms, especially swearing and facial grimaces, are done for social approval. These mannerisms can often be quickly changed when they are ignored or when they meet with disapproval rather than approval.

Unfortunately, many physical mannerisms are intrinsically rewarding, such as squirming and mouth noises. A well-designed sequence of physical punishment might reduce the specific mannerisms that are punished, but as suggested earlier, most parents are not willing to spend the time and effort needed for such a technique. Perhaps the best discipline techniques are gentle but persistent reminders in the form of mild physical punishment, such as a gentle slap on the hand as it probes in the nose, combined with psychological punishment such as, "That's a filthy habit; don't you know better?" These forms of punishment should also be combined with other explanations and reasoning, such as, "You should go in the bathroom and get a tissue," or "You should turn away from the table and use your handkerchief."

**Laziness.** The sixth cause of misbehavior is laziness or dawdling. Some children seem to have enormous difficulty getting anything done, even the most simple activities, such as dressing themselves, eating their meals, or picking up their toys. This form of dawdling is often caused by mental distractions; the child may be engrossed in fantasies and thoughts that are far more exciting than such mundane things as eating or dressing. This form of misbehavior is caused by forgetfulness more than it is caused by laziness, and you need to spend a lot of time providing gentle reminders.

Laziness in children is caused by a lack of motivation, and motivation is created by the kinds of rewards or punishments associated with the performance. Sometimes children fail to perform a task because there are no rewards for doing so. "Why should I change the light bulb in the downstairs bathroom when I never use it?" Other times they fail to perform a task because the job is punishing. "I don't want to weed the flower beds; it's hard work." Still other times they fail to accomplish the task because there are competing activities that are more enticing. "I didn't want to do the dishes because my favorite TV program came on."

As explained in chapter 7, if parents want to motivate children they need to provide sufficient rewards. Whether they use positive rewards for good performance or punishment for failure to perform, parents must somehow make sure that the consequences for performing the task are more desirable than the consequences of failing to perform it. This reality is very disappointing to parents who would like to see their children internally motivated to do good things without the parents having to reward or punish. Over a long period of time, children acquire intrinsic rewards that will motivate them to perform on their own. But while these intrinsic rewards and work values are being acquired, you will need to play a very active role in providing positive rewards and encouragement. The techniques you should use in solving problems of laziness were described in chapters 7 and 8. Skillful parents are able to motivate children effectively by various combinations of both positive rewards and natural and imposed consequences.

**Willful disobedience.** The seventh cause of misbehavior is willful disobedience. Here the child consciously behaves contrary to the parents' express commands. No doubt every child occasionally refuses to obey, but some parents think willful disobedience accounts for over 90 percent of their children's misbehavior. These parents need to carefully assess whether their own behavior contributes to the problem. For example, when parents say "Turn off the television; it's almost bedtime," the real message is, "Okay, kids, you've only got another fifteen or twenty minutes." Both parents and children know from past experience that the first comment was only a flippant warning. The parents did not really expect the children to move, and the children knew it. Not until the same instruction is repeated the third time in a much louder and more threatening voice does the message to turn off the television become a real command. At that point, they turn it off obediently and wonder why the parents are so upset. In the children's eyes, they were not guilty of willful disobedience.

There are dramatic differences in the degree of willful disobedience in children, and you need to tailor the discipline to fit the disobedience. Failing to turn off the television and come to dinner is quite different than cruelly teasing a younger child contrary to repeated instructions to stop.

The imposition of parental power is generally appropriate when dealing with willful disobedience. The parents could have obtained much better obedience, for example, if they had turned off the television themselves and then announced it was bedtime. Having the child sit on a chair, forego desired privileges, or write an essay on the correct way to behave can also be effective, especially when the child has time to think about what he did wrong and how he should have behaved. If they are not used excessively or harshly, power assertive techniques are useful because they get the child's attention and condition the child to be more attentive in the future. Many times the reason for willful misbehavior is because the child did not pay adequate attention to the parents' commands.

The most serious form of willful disobedience is a defiant, disrespectful, and verbally abusive challenge to the parent. This extreme form of disobedience is where physical punishment is not only useful but desirable. The physical pain communicates to the child that he made a mistake and that the parents' authority needs to be honored. Harsh whippings are never appropriate, and there is no need to use anything that would inflict greater pain than most parents can inflict with their hand. A few solid strokes should be sufficient to produce genuine tears on the outside and a different disposition on the inside. But, spankings should be used very sparingly. Frequent spankings are ineffective and generally suggest that parents are failing to administer other forms of discipline effectively.

Respect for the authority of parents needs to be established early. Many of the early philosophers of the seventeenth and eighteenth centuries clearly taught that respect for authority should be established within the first year or two of a child's life. Afterwards, only gentle and infrequent reminders are needed. To their great dismay, many parents realize that after a child reaches twelve to fourteen years of age, the usefulness of physical punishment is virtually gone. After this age, parents have to rely on other marginally effective power-assertive techniques, such as grounding children or confining them to their room, combined with large doses of induction to deal with willful disobedience. Most parents report a perplexing paradox in administering discipline: discipline is least effective on the child that needs it the most. The more discipline a child needs, the less good the discipline does.

Parents cannot rely on physical punishment to establish or maintain their authority. Your role as a parent gives you some authority to influence your children; but the real basis for your authority comes from the love and respect you engender in your child. Parents earn the respect of their children by being effective role models and by treating them with reciprocal love and respect.

Thus, the most useful discipline techniques for handling willful disobedience include punishment combined with a lot of teaching and modeling. You need to be an effective model showing love and respect for others, especially for the child; and the induction needs to contain logical explanations for your commands along with a justification of why and when children should submit to authority. The reason why punishment must occur in an atmosphere of love is discussed later.

## Summary

*Natural and logical consequences are more effective than imposed consequences, and parents need to identify the natural consequences associated with their children's misbehavior.*

*Psychological punishment and withholding love are poor discipli-
nary techniques that fail to teach moral values, although they
may induce feelings of guilt.*

*Physical punishment and other power assertive techniques do not
teach moral values and are generally ineffective in suppressing undesirable behavior unless they are mild, consistent, and
administered immediately after the misbehavior.*

*Induction and modeling are valuable, if not necessary, processes
of moral development because they help the child internalize
acceptable values during the discipline encounter.*

*Parents may appropriately display their emotions when disciplin-
ing their child, provided their emotions are mature feelings
and not anger or hatred toward the child.*

*The correct disciplinary action depends on the cause of the dis-
obedience; e.g., physical discomfort, curiosity, carelessness,
forgetfulness, objectionable mannerisms, laziness, and willful
disobedience. Physical punishment is appropriate and even
desirable when the child is defiant and willfully disobedient.*

# 10

# Parental
# Influence

How much influence should you exert over your children? Should children be allowed to do whatever they want, or should you guide and control their activities? Almost daily, parents find themselves trying to decide how actively they should be involved in their children's lives. These daily dilemmas often leave parents feeling guilty because they feel they could have done more to be good parents. When confrontations occur between parents and children or when children misbehave, the parents often feel guilty and accept the problems as their own personal failures.

If you experience these painful feelings of disappointment and despair, you need to remember that your children have their own personal agency and that as parents you cannot control them entirely. You can only influence, persuade, and direct; you do not have absolute control and you cannot deprive your children of their agency. If you do a good job, however, you can be reasonably confident of being able to raise socially responsible, well-behaved children. "Train up a child in the way he

should go:  and when he is old, he will not depart from it"
(Proverbs 22:6).

## Freedom Versus Control

How much influence should parents exert in directing and
controlling the lives of their children?  This question has been
debated extensively, and a variety of opinions have been offered.
Some people have argued that children should be entirely free of
parental influence and allowed to live in an unrestricted environment.  Others have argued just the opposite, that parents have a
responsibility to carefully guide and control their children's
behavior.  This issue has generated enormous controversy, and
the correct answer depends largely on the age and maturity of the
child.  Young children need to be directed and controlled, while
older children should be allowed to direct their lives with only
limited parental control.  The arguments used in the freedom versus control controversy  help to explain the proper balance of
parental influence.

At the end of the continuum is the philosophy usually
ascribed to Jean-Jacques Rousseau (1712-1778), an eighteenth
century philosopher, who argued that children are like a blank
sheet of paper, unspoiled and unpolluted.  Like the noble savage,
Rousseau argued, children will mature best if they are left alone
to follow a natural course.  Rousseau condemned civilization for
corrupting the basic goodness of human nature.  This philosophy
was adopted by A.S. Neill, the director of Summerhill School in
England, who advocated total independence for children to do
anything they wanted without adult intrusion.

Summerhill School was founded in 1921 in the village of
Leiston, about one hundred miles from London.  The school usually had between sixty and seventy students who ranged in ages
from five to eighteen and were housed at the school.  The main
objective in the design of Summerhill was to make the school fit
the child's needs.  The children were ostensibly free to "be them-

selves" through the elimination of all discipline, all direction, and all moral and religious training. Lessons were scheduled in the morning only, but they were entirely optional and the children could decide when, if ever, they wanted to attend school  Some children chose to never attend school and actually stayed away from classes for several years. There were no exams, no grades, and no scheduled assignments. The goal of Summerhill was not to educate the children, but to make them happy and loving individuals. Neill argued, however, that the academic performances of many students were not significantly inferior to other children who went through public schools.

Since becoming a loving person was the only real goal of Summerhill, there were essentially no required behaviors demanded of the students. Not only could they miss class indefinitely; they were not required to make their bed, clean their room, wash themselves, or perform household duties. There were also very few restricted behaviors of things they could not do. The children were required to follow only a few rules, primarily concerning safety precautions, which were passed by a majority vote in a general school meeting. Other behavioral problems, such as muddy feet in the parlor, were handled through interpersonal negotiation between equals, since there were no positions of authority.

Neill's description gives the initial impression that he and his staff exerted virtually no influence on the children's behavior. However, they learned from experience that additional restraints were necessary, such as locking the workshop, the theater, and the pottery shop to keep students out; and some behaviors could not be tolerated, such as noise after bedtime hours, using other people's belongings without permission, and being destructive. Nevertheless, to a radical extreme each individual was free to do what he wanted as long as he was not trespassing on the freedom of others.

Neill's permissive educational philosophy is described in his book, *Summerhill,* in which he encouraged parents to adopt the same permissive approach to raise children.[34] Children should be totally free to develop naturally not only at school but also in the home. He instructed parents to take a stance of noninterference regarding scholastic achievement, social development, morality, religion, and everything else except physical safety.

Neill's belief in the inherent goodness of children and his recommendation that they be given absolute freedom have been severely criticized. After ten years of intense controversy, the publisher of *Summerhill* asked a group of educators, ministers, and behavioral scientists to evaluate Neill's philosophy. Some of the reviews were positive, but most were very critical. A Jesuit priest thought Neill's philosophy was an inspired concept and called the Summerhill school a "holy place." A state superintendent of public instruction, however, condemned Neill's philosophy and said he would rather enroll his child in a brothel than in Summerhill. A research director of a child development institute said Neill was like a small, bad boy who had never gotten over his own boyhood rebellion and was continually and blatantly thumbing his nose at society. The English School Inspectors' report praised the dedication of the headmaster, Neill, but said that the overall results of the system and the quality of the teaching were both unimpressive, that the children lacked guidance, that Summerhill was a difficult place in which to study, and that the students' achievements were meager.[35]

A.S. Neill's radical, permissive philosophy is not recommended by most of the popular child-rearing books. Even the most permissive authors of popular child-rearing literature realize that parents must be more actively involved in influencing their children's behavior. Haim Ginott, author of the popular book *Between Parent and Child*, argues that parents should direct their children's choices.[36] Children should be deliberately presented with many situations in which they have to make choices; but the parents select the situation, and the children then make the choices. Ginott specifically recommended that children be allowed to choose which foods to eat and clothes to wear. Regarding homework he said that parents should never supervise it or check it. Homework is strictly the responsibility of the child and his teacher. Ginott carefully avoided taking sides on whether parents should insist that their children develop musical talent. While he praised music as an excellent emotional outlet, he said that children should not be nagged about practicing. In short, Ginott advocated giving children considerable latitude over their own activities, subject to a minimum of limiting constraints such as, "Is it helpful, safe, and within our budget?"

In the first edition of *Baby and Child Care* (1946), Dr. Benjamin Spock recommended a very permissive approach to child rearing.[37] In later editions, however, he reversed his position and advocated a much more active role for parents in raising their children. Spock told parents that is was their responsibility to teach their children good manners and have them perform household duties. All children, he argued, need to be guided, reminded, and corrected no matter how well disposed they are— that is the parents' job. He said that good parents who naturally lean towards strictness should stick to their guns and raise their children that way. Moderate strictness in the sense of requiring good manners, prompt obedience, and orderliness is not harmful to children as long as parents are basically kind and as long as the children are growing up happy and friendly. Strictness, he said, was harmful only when the parents were overbearing, harsh, chronically disapproving, and made no allowances for the child's age and individuality.

One of the most enthusiastic proponents of discipline is James Dobson, author of *Dare to Discipline*.[38] Dobson attributed much of the deterioration in the attitudes and behavior of youth—drug abuse, abortion, school dropouts, and juvenile delinquency—to the inadequacy of discipline in the homes and schools. Parents falsely assumed, he claimed, that they only needed to supply affection and material needs in a permissive atmosphere. Permissiveness has not just been a failure, he said, it's been a disaster. He attributed most of the problem to a lack of discipline during the tender years of childhood when parents demanded neither respect nor responsible behavior from their children. As a consequence, the children failed to develop the self-control and self-discipline that were needed to help them become responsible individuals.

## Intrusive Child Rearing

Most of the prominent theologians and philosophers of the seventeenth, eighteenth, and nineteenth centuries taught parents that it was their responsibility to demand strict obedience and teach their children self-discipline and self-control. This philosophy has been called an "intrusive" philosophy of child rearing because parents literally intrude into every aspect of the child's life.

This intrusive philosophy appears to have been very prominent among the large population of middle- and lower-class people, especially those who were religious. John Locke (1632-1704) said that most parents make a serious mistake by failing to discipline the minds of their children early enough. He felt the problem with disobedient children was "that the mind has not been made obedient to discipline, and pliant to reason, when at first it was most tender, most easy to be bowed."[39] Like the shaping of a tree, it must be done while it is young and pliable. If young children are given grapes or sugar plums every time they are out of humor, Locke asked, why wouldn't they demand to have their desires for wine or women satisfied when they are older? "The difference lies not in having or not having appetites, but in the power to govern and deny ourselves in them. He that is not used to submit his will to the reason of others, when he is young, will scarce hearken or submit to his own reason when he is of an age to make use of it."[40]

The idea that parents have a critical responsibility to form the minds of their children while they are young was espoused by many other authors in both America and Europe, including John Robinson (1575-1625), Cotton Mather (1663-1728), John Witherspoon (1723-1794), Jonathan Edwards (1703-1758), and Susanna Wesley (1670-1742).[41] John Witherspoon was a college president (Princeton College), clergyman, and statesman (the only clergyman to sign the Declaration of Independence). In his letters on education, Witherspoon explained why absolute authority in raising young children was necessary. "I have said above, that you should establish as soon as possible an entire and absolute authority. I would have it early, that it may be absolute, and absolute, that it may not be severe. If parents are too long in the beginning to exert their authority, they will find the task very difficult. Children, habituated to indulgence for a few of their first years, are exceedingly impatient of restraint; and if they happen to be of stiff or obstinate tempers, can hardly be brought to an entire, at least to a quieter and placid submission; whereas, if they are taken in time, there is hardly any temper but what may be made to yield, and by early habit the subjection becomes quite easy to themselves."[42]

Thus, during the seventeenth, eighteenth, and nineteenth centuries, parents were admonished to exert an enormous amount of influence over their children's lives. This influence was supposed to start as soon as a child was old enough to comprehend it. For small things, like crying for toys or sweets, the influence was supposed to start as soon as the child was a year old. For other behaviors, such as self-control, sexual purity, and family chores, the influence of parents extended through adolescence and into adulthood. This intrusive philosophy taught by educators, philosophers, and religious leaders was the dominant social norm in America. In following this advice, parents generally disciplined and controlled their children in a compassionate, humanitarian way that showed concern for the emotional well-being of the child. In some instances, harsh discipline resulted in cruel and inhumane treatment of children, even though it was usually well intended. But as a general rule, parents learned that firm discipline administered by concerned parents created socially responsible children who were happy and well behaved.

## Parenting Crisis

Because of the freedom-versus-control controversy, you can expect to face some critical difficulties in exercising your parental authority. When your children are young, you need to exert a strong influence over their behavior and demand obedience. But as they mature, you should allow them to be more independent. Children should gradually learn to act for themselves and to make their own decisions.

Consider the following situation: suppose your child wanted to watch a special Christmas program on television one Saturday evening. You expect the program to be a good show and it meets with your approval, but because of unforeseen scheduling problems the program will be broadcast at a late hour. Should you allow your child to watch this program? The answer depends on the age of your child more than the lateness of the hour. The appropriate response would be much different if the child were six, twelve, or eighteen years old. For the six-year-old, you should make the decision. For the twelve-year-old, the decision should be jointly decided by both you and your child. Most eighteen-year-olds would make this decision alone, without even asking permission.

As a parent, you exert almost complete control over a new born baby, and for the next five or six years you should relinquish very little of this influence. During these early years, you need to influence almost every part of your children's lives: what they eat, what they wear, how they spend their time, what time they go to bed, how often they bathe, how they wear their hair, what is an acceptable vocabulary, and how they behave when they get upset. Gradually you need to give them more freedom to decide things for themselves. Giving them too much freedom too fast contributes to irresponsible behavior, yet being too slow to allow them to make their own decisions creates anger and rebelliousness.

Most parents face a crisis sometime when their children are between the ages of twelve and sixteen. The children have been gradually exercising greater freedom by making small decisions about their behavior, and they come to expect total freedom and complete noninterference from their parents. Most parents, however, are not willing to allow their children to enjoy such freedom, and they still believe it is their responsibility to make many of the major decisions in their children's lives. Some parents are not willing to relinquish any of their authority until they reach a major impasse when their authority is seriously threatened or undermined.

This crisis is often accompanied by intense emotion and conflict. In these situations, both you and your child need great maturity. Children need to be patient and realize that they cannot mature overnight, and you need to realize that you can no longer make all decisions for your children. Your responsibility switches from one of controlling and directing your children's lives to helping them become independent and able to act for themselves. You should now serve as a resource for recommending solutions and offering advice. Your children may or may not accept your advice, but if they are mature and responsible young adults they will always ask for your advice and at least consider it carefully.

## Consequences of Too Little Discipline

As a parent, you are responsible for establishing guidelines of acceptable behavior, communicating them to your children, and enforcing compliance with them. You need to demand strict obedience to standards of right and wrong, especially with younger children. Sometimes it is difficult, however, to know how strict you really must be, because even the best children occasionally violate the standards. You can expect to ask yourself on many occasions when you see your children misbehave, "Should I do something about it or just overlook it?" Sometimes you don't need to do anything. If you try to respond to every misbehavior, you may find yourself constantly nagging your children and creating a repressive and unpleasant environment. Furthermore, children frequently know when they have misbehaved, and they may resolve to do better next time without you saying anything or even raising an eyebrow.

What are the consequences of too little discipline by parents? What happens when you fail to set standards or allow children to violate the standards without saying or doing anything? What are the symptoms of insufficient discipline?

The purpose of discipline is to create responsible and mature individuals. Discipline is not something you do *to* children, but something you do *for* them. Some of the consequences of inadequate discipline were discussed in chapter 3. When you fail to set appropriate standards of behavior or allow children to disobey them, children fail to learn the rules of the game; they are not aware of the physical constraints and social norms governing their behavior; nor do they appreciate the standards expected of them. Consequently, they do not feel free, since freedom consists in part of an appreciation of necessity. In other words, children are able to free themselves from the outside world by understanding its natural laws and controlling their reactions to what happens. This definition equates the concept of freedom with the power to act rather than the absence of external controls.

So why can't children be free? Children are not free by virtue of their ignorance of physical and social realities, their dependence upon others for sustenance, their lack of experience, and their lack of self-control. As children develop greater self-control and become more independent in making responsible decisions and accepting responsibility for their own behavior, they should obtain greater freedom from their parents. Their newfound freedom does not mean they will behave contrary to their parents' desires; in fact, the reason they should be granted such freedom is because they have convinced their parents they will make wise choices consistent with what the parents would have chosen themselves.

It is interesting to note that in the studies of high-risk families reported by Blum and his associates (see chapter 3), the children of the high-risk families did not feel free even though one of the major child-rearing goals of their parents was for their children to be independent and act for themselves. These high-risk children reported that they felt constrained on every hand by rules that were inconsistently imposed within the home, rules within the school, rules in the community, and oppressive social norms. Apparently the permissive practices of their parents failed to help the children obtain an appreciation of the natural laws imposed on them in their environment, and they lacked the self-control to make responsible decisions.

An unfortunate consequence of too little parental discipline is a lack of self-respect within the child. A loss of self-respect within children is a serious consequence, since this also extends to a loss of respect for other people and social institutions. To love others and appreciate social institutions, children must feel good about themselves. But if children have failed to develop self-respect and self-control, they will not have positive self-esteem.

Self-esteem is a function of how you evaluate yourself. A child's self-esteem is largely determined by what he or she does. You may try to help your children have higher levels of self-esteem by complimenting them and telling them that they are great and wonderful. Children are fully aware of what they have done, however, and this "brag 'em up" approach will not increase a child's self-esteem nearly as much as helping the child develop greater knowledge, skills, and self-discipline, which will enable him or her to do good things. Children who do good things are proud of their performance and have positive self-esteem.

One of the first evidences of inadequate discipline is defiant rebelliousness. When parents fail to set appropriate standards of behavior or tolerate disobedience, children begin to develop their own standards of behavior, which are usually based on what is fun and easy rather than on what is right. This defiance is often observed in the lives of young children at the ages of two and three. Some youngsters can be very obstinate and headstrong: they refuse to eat the food prepared for them, they refuse to wear certain clothes, they refuse to go to bed on time, or they make trivial and unreasonable demands.

The time when young children are openly defiant is the time for parents to exert firm discipline. When a defiant nose-to-nose confrontation occurs between you and your child, this is not the time to have an intellectual discussion about the virtues of obedience. If you have developed the rules well in advance and clearly communicated them, and your youngster responds in stiffnecked rebellion with a defiant "I will not" or "You shut up," this is the time for you to exert firm discipline. Spankings are generally reserved for such times of willful disobedience. It is not necessary to beat the child into submission. A little pain goes a long way for a young child. However, the spanking should be hard enough to cause the child to cry genuinely. After a few tears the child will often want to fall into your arms, and he should be welcomed with open, warm, and loving arms. At that moment you can talk with your child heart to heart and tell him how much you love him and how important he is to you. You can also explain why he was punished and how to avoid difficulty in the future. Parents who defend spanking claim that other disciplinary techniques, such as sitting children in the corner or sending them to their rooms, do not provide the same meaningful learning experience.

## Abuse of Parental Power

One of the greatest scriptural insights regarding leadership says that "no power or influence can or ought to be maintained by virtue of the priesthood, only by persuasion, by long-suffering, by gentleness and meekness, and by love unfeigned; by kindness, and pure knowledge, which shall greatly enlarge the soul without hypocrisy, and without guile—reproving betimes with sharpness, when moved upon by the Holy Ghost; and then showing forth afterwards an increase of love toward him whom thou has reproved, lest he esteem thee to be his enemy" (Doctrine and Covenants 121:41-43).

Applying this scripture to parents' authority indicates that parents should not maintain power and authority simply because they are the parents. It is true that parents are responsible for teaching and disciplining their children. Children should respect their parents, and parents ought to expect their children to respect them. But parents should not exercise arbitrary power and expect their children to obey simply because they are the parents.

Parental authority can be established on three foundations: first, parents have a legal responsibility to raise their children and exercise authority over them. Until the child reaches age eighteen, parents have the authority to guide and supervise their children's behavior. Second, the authority of parents is established by the moral obligations of parents to care for their children. This obligation to care for their children is accompanied by the right to expect obedience and respect from children. This moral foundation is clearly taught in the scriptures, although it was much more popularly accepted before 1900 than today. "Honour thy father and thy mother" (Exodus 20:12). "Children, obey your parents in the Lord: for this is right" (Ephesians 6:1). Finally, the authority of parents is founded on a rational, legitimate authority base. Parents are the leaders of a family, and, like the leaders of any organization, social norms bestow upon leaders the legitimate right to exert influence on subordinates.

In spite of these three authority bases, however, you should not attempt to maintain power and influence over children simply because you are the parents. When the father tells his son to mow the lawn and the son protests, the father should not assume that the fact that he is the father is a sufficient justification for him to exert influence. It may be true that he is the father, and it may also be true that he has the responsibility for delegating family chores. Both the father and the son should realize that there are other legitimate reasons why the son should mow the lawn and that the father is not just exercising power arbitrarily.

Remember that no power or influence can or ought to be *maintained* by virtue of an individual's position. The key word is *maintained*. At times you may be required to act rapidly and decisively, especially when the safety or security of your children are at stake. Nevertheless, you should always ask yourself, "Are there rational reasons and legitimate justifications for exerting this influence, or is it just an exercise of power on my part?" Arbitrary demands without any legitimate justification are illustrations of unrighteous dominion. Parental authority must be maintained by love and respect, and parents must behave in a way that preserves and enhances this love and respect.

*Losing your temper.* Learning to control your temper and govern your emotions is as great a challenge for parents as it is for children. When asked what is the greatest challenge in raising their children, many parents admit that they fail to control their temper as well as they should. If you are sincerely trying to raise socially responsible children, you can expect many disappointments when you see your children misbehave. The interesting paradox is that the more you care about your children's behavior, the more intense will be your feelings of disappointment. Even the best children are not perfect. If you didn't care about your children, it would be easier for you to control your temper.

The best time to learn emotional control is not when you are angry. When your body is full of adrenalin and your emotions are racing hot, you are almost certain to respond in the same way you've responded to similar situations in the past. If you have a habit of running around yelling, screaming, and threatening when your emotions run high, you will have a difficult time behaving differently unless you have prepared in advance. Learning to control your temper occurs during times when you are calm and rational and you can objectively assess how you feel about your behavior and decide how you ought to behave. During the times when you are calm, you need to think carefully about the proper way to respond and develop a detailed and realistic plan for responding on future occasions. If your plans are sufficiently clear and precise, you will have a greater chance of responding appropriately the next time you are upset. Most parents believe there are legitimate reasons for being upset, and it is easy to justify their storming and condemning. After they have calmed down, however, they realize that their emotional outburst did not improve the situation; it only created greater barriers and a loss of respect with their child.

*Habit of saying no.* Some parents are overly restrictive and get in the habit of saying no to every request their children make. Occasionally this habit develops because parents fail to involve themselves adequately in their children's lives. Rather than deciding what their children ought to do and actively helping them, the parents ignore their children's needs and arbitrarily deny every request. On many occasions it is appropriate to say no; but if you find yourself saying no too often, you ought to ask yourself whether you have developed a habit of saying no without thinking. One method of breaking this habit is to force yourself to offer a compromise activity before you arbitrarily say no.

*Child abuse.* Perhaps the most serious abuse of parental power occurs when parents verbally, physically or sexually abuse their children. Physical child abuse involves extreme physical treatment that results in visible injury to the child. Such injuries might include single or multiple cuts, fractures, burns, bruises, or other symptoms that are encompassed by the "battered child syndrome." The severity and frequency of child abuse have been absolutely alarming. Estimates of child abuse in the United States alone have ranged from 500,000 to 2 million families per year. These shocking statistics have prompted many states to require that suspected cases of child abuse be reported and investigated. Where child abuse is confirmed, parents are often required to cooperate with a welfare worker in following a plan of rehabilitation for parents and children.

The incidence of sexual abuse within families is also shocking; and it is generally believed that the number of reported cases represents such a small part of the overall problem that it is difficult to estimate. Sexual abuse can be committed by either parent against children of either sex, although it appears to be most frequently committed by fathers against their own daughters.

Both physical and sexual child abuse are serious problems that can leave intense emotional scars in the memories of children. Some instances of child abuse are committed by parents with a mental disorder who consciously and intentionally plan and carry out their abusive acts. Some parents may not actually commit an abusive act but spend an inordinate amount of time fantasizing and planning in their mind how they might abuse their children. These individuals need professional psychiatric counseling to help them develop a healthier attitude toward themselves and their families.

Most instances of physical and sexual abuse, however, are not premeditated and consciously planned. They occur on the spur of the moment when feelings of lust or anger go unchecked. To prevent these situations from happening, parents need to have firmly established rules in their mind regarding their own behavior. For example, parents may need to make their own personal rule to the effect that no matter how angry or upset they become with their child, they will never act on an immediate impulse to punish the child. For example, some parents have rules that they never spank a child anywhere but on their upper legs and rear end. Other parents have a rule that they will never spank their children until after they have looked them in the eye and told them why they are getting spanked.

To avoid problems of sexual abuse, parents need to carefully guard their thoughts and behaviors. Parents need to avoid seductive fantasies and lurid conversations with their children. There is nothing wrong with parents being affectionate and loving with their children. In fact, an affectionate hugging and kissing association between parents and children of either sex is quite appropriate even during their adolescent years. But parents need to avoid indecent exposure or inappropriate touching of either themselves or their children, and make a conscious effort to respect personal modesty and privacy.

There is a significant difference between sexual abuse and an affectionate, loving relationship between parent and child. Being affectionate and loving does not lead to sexual abuse if parents have the proper understanding of the meaning and role of love and sex.

Likewise, there is a significant difference between physical punishment and physical child abuse. Spanking children at appropriate times does not necessarily lead to child abuse. To avoid physical child abuse, parents need to make certain that they never vent their frustrations on their child or lose control of their emotions.

## Summary

*Although some child-rearing experts tell parents to avoid influencing their children, others encourage parents to be very active in directing their children's lives. Earlier philosophers especially advocated an intrusive approach to raising children.*

*When children are young, parents need to play an active, intrusive role in guiding their children's lives. But as children mature, parents need to encourage children to be more independent and to make their own decisions.*

*Parents and children typically experience an authority crisis in early teenage years as children want to assume greater autonomy and parents want to maintain control. A lack of self-respect and self-discipline, and an increase in resistiveness and rebelliousness, are typically indications of insufficient parental discipline.*

*Parents abuse their parental authority by acting arbitrarily, losing their temper, developing the habit of saying no, and physically or sexually abusing their child.*

# 11

# Building
# Better Relationships

John Locke (1632-1704) offered the following advice to fathers:

> Would you have your son obedient to you, when past a child?
> Be sure to establish the authority of a father, as soon as he is capa-
> ble of submission, and can understand in whose power he is. If you
> would have him stand in awe of you, imprint it in his infancy; and,
> as he approaches more to a man, admit him nearer to your famil-
> iarity: so shall you have him your obedient subject (as is fit) whilst
> he is a child, and your affectionate friend when he is a man. For
> methinks they mightily misplace the treatment due to their chil-
> dren, who are indulgent and familiar when they are little, but severe
> to them, and keep them at a distance when they are grown up. For
> liberty and indulgence can do no good to children: their want of
> judgment makes them stand in need of restraint and discipline. . . .
> Fear and awe ought to give you the first power over their minds,
> and love and friendship in riper years to hold it: for the time must
> come, when they will be past the rod of correction; and then, if the
> love of you make them not obedient and dutiful; if the love of
> virtue and reputation keep them not in laudable courses; I ask, what
> hold will you have upon them?[43]

This advice from John Locke, written in 1690, describes the need for a combination of discipline in the earlier years and friendship in later years. When children are young, you need to establish firm expectations of acceptable behavior and demand strict obedience to them. When your children become teenagers, however, the same disciplinary techniques will not be effective, nor are they appropriate. Hopefully they learned to be obedient when they were young and they are ready to accept more personal responsibility. During their teenage years is the time to build a relationship that will endure after they reach adulthood. As they mature, their relationship with you should change from seeing you as absolute authority to seeing you as their best and closest friend. Just as you would not choose someone to be your friend if he constantly created an unpleasant relationship, so also will your grown children avoid you if you continually rebuke, browbeat, and maintain an unpleasant interpersonal relationship.

Building a relationship with teenagers is not an easy task because there are so many changes and uncertainties in their lives. Their feelings can change rapidly from day to day regardless of what you do; their self-esteem is not stable and may fluctuate widely; and they may treat you very respectfully and obediently one day and disrespectfully and discourteously the next. Sometimes the relationships between parents and teenagers become so toxic that the parents feel a total loss in knowing where to begin building the relationship. Although it may not be easy, there are several techniques parents can use to build a better relationship.

## Patience and Persistence

Parents need to be patient and persistent regardless of their children's ages, but these virtues are particularly important for building a relationship with teenagers. Patiently and persistently, you need to continually encourage them to be obedient and to make wise decisions regardless of how often they misbehave. If you are nasty and condemning every time you correct them, they will feel browbeaten and defeated. But if you are tactful and polite and simply try to let them know you have higher expectations and hope they will behave better in the future, your gentle encouragement will eventually have an impact.

In the game of raising teenage children, parents can lose a lot of battles and still win the war. The following illustration demonstrates how you can continually lose confrontation after confrontation with your children and still succeed in achieving your major objectives.

"Dad died when I was eleven. I was the third of six children. My oldest brother Tom, who was fourteen, was determined no one would ever take Dad's place. I never really understood why Tom was against grownups, but he had us convinced that if we listened to other grownups it mean that we didn't respect Dad. I know it's really silly now, but for several years we didn't listen to anything grownups told us. It didn't matter whether they were our teachers, our neighbors, our bishop, or the police. Because we were so stubborn, we turned out to be real troublemakers for the next few years. Mom was always working and didn't have time to control us. She was usually so worn out when she came home, she didn't have the energy to fight with us. Our house was always a mess—you wouldn't believe the basement. The entire floor was covered with four or five inches of clothes. People were always bringing sacks of clothes their kids had outgrown because they knew we were poor. We never turned them down, of course, but no one could sort through them and take care of them. They were just thrown all over the floor.

"After being alone for several years, Mother remarried in spite of our protests. We decided we weren't going to like him. Instead of calling him Dad, we always called him Harold. When he joined our family he was the only one who didn't shout and scream at other people. He was always tactful and calm, and we thought we could railroad over him any time we wanted. I didn't think he would stay more than a couple of weeks because of the way we treated him. At the time I thought he lost every argument he ever had with us. But looking back on it now, I realize he was the winner. Instead of driving him out, he succeeded in changing us.

"One of the first times I learned to listen to Harold was when we had the sailboat accident. We were vacationing at a lake, and two of us wanted to take the sailboat out when we saw the wind pick up. Harold told us we shouldn't go out because a heavy storm was coming from the south. We could see the dark clouds and we knew it was a storm, but we weren't going to let Harold tell us what to do. When he saw how defiant we were, I expected him to crack down hard and refuse to let us go. Instead, he simply cautioned us and told us to stay in the bay where we would be safer.

"Instead of following his advice, we sailed out of the bay to ride on stronger winds. When the storm finally hit, we were in real trouble. Harold must have known we were going to have trouble because he reached us in a motor boat a few minutes after we capsized. In spite of our embarrassment we were really glad to see him. There was no way we could have gotten the sailboat upright in the water; the mast was pointing straight down. We expected a lecture on disobedience; instead all Harold said was the obvious fact, 'You're lucky you didn't lose the boat.'

"Whenever we wanted to do something Harold didn't want us to do, he'd keep telling us why we shouldn't do it. Sometimes he'd spend hours going over the same reasons again and again. We could tell how important it was to him, because the more important it was the longer he'd keep talking. He never came right out and refused to let us go; he kept saying it was our decision. But if we didn't decide what he wanted us to decide, he'd just keep talking. Sometimes we gave in just so he would shut up, but most of the time we did what we wanted anyway, and sure enough, we'd usually find out that he was right—just like with the sailboat accident. We shouldn't have gone out that day, or at least we should have stayed in the bay.

"It took a long time for him to change us, but I have to take my hat off to him now. We really respect him, even though we still call him Harold."

In time, Harold was remarkably successful in helping the children behave responsibly even though he appeared to lose every confrontation with them. His patience and persistence helped him succeed in the end. If you are patient, you will have greater success in maintaining open lines of communication and your children will listen to you. If you are also persistent, you will gradually succeed in creating responsible children and helping them internalize the values you cherish. You do not need to win every confrontation with your children. In fact, many times you need to give in to their desires and simply let them know what you expect and that you hope the future will be better. Read the following two situations, for example:

- "Listen, Kent, I know you want to go to the mall with your friends, and I'm sure it would be a lot of fun. But you haven't finished your homework yet, and there are other things you need to do. Even though I don't think you should go, I'm not going to make this decision for you. You're fourteen years old and you need to decide this one for yourself. You know how important it is to get good grades, and we both know that fooling around at the mall is not as important as some of the other things you could spend your time doing."
- "Tamara, I reminded you three times last night to pick up your Barbie dolls before you went to bed, and then I reminded you again this morning before you went to school. You didn't get

it done, and so I had to pick them up before I could vacuum the family room. When you're through playing with your toys you need to take care of them. That's part of your responsibility."

Obviously Kent's father could have insisted that he stay home and do his homework rather than go to the mall with his friends, and Tammy's mother could have phoned the second grade teacher and had Tammy sent home to pick up her dolls. Occasionally you may want to escalate the confrontation and fight to the end just so your children know how important obedience is to you. It is not necessary, however, to win every confrontation. Occasionally you gain more by losing because it provides an opportunity for you to talk with your children and patiently explain where they have failed and why you feel so strongly that they need to behave differently.

## Avoiding Impasses

What do you do when you reach an impasse with your children? You say yes; they say no. They insist on going; you refuse to let them go. As noted earlier, how such disciplinary encounters are resolved should depend considerably on the child's age. Parents should exert much firmer influence during the earlier years than when the child is a teenager.

Regardless of the child's age, parents should assess the strength of their positions and think twice before they create an impasse situation. Don't allow yourself to get locked into a win-lose situation unless you know you are right and the issue is worth fighting for. Even then you may want to avoid the impasse situation, not because you are wrong or you might lose, but because losing can be destructive to your child.   In win-lose situations, both parties typically lose. Even when one person appears to be the decisive winner, the confrontation damages the relationship. You will not find much satisfaction in the long-term consequences that come from continually defeating your children.

The best way to handle an impasse is obviously to avoid it.

Try to find alternatives in which both parties may win. If children don't like spinach, rather than forcing them to eat it maybe they could be persuaded to have one small bite. In time they may learn to like it, and in the meantime they can eat other vegetables.

Parents can prevail in some impasse situations because of their size and superior intellect. If the child wants to do something contrary to the parents' wishes, parents can usually employ physical force to prevent them from doing it. If they don't want them to ride their bike, they can hide the bike. If they don't want them to eat candy, they can take the candy away. If they don't want them to leave the house or play in the street, they can bolt the doors or otherwise physically restrain them.

There are other impasse situations, however, where parents cannot win regardless of their size and experience. If children adamantly refuse to do something, parents may find there is nothing they can do to force them to do it. Children at any age can successfully refuse to eat something they don't want to. Many frustrated mothers have pried their child's mouth open and stuffed food in only to see it spit back out. At a family reunion, a father saw his five-year-old son retaliate against a cousin who had been teasing him. The retaliation resulted in a tussle in which the parents finally intervened. The father told his son to apologize, but his son felt that he should be the recipient, not the giver, of an apology. After insisting ever more loudly that his son apologize, he finally threatened to spank his son if he didn't say he was sorry. Finally the father decided that his son's refusal was embarrassing him in front of his family, but neither the first mild spanking nor the second firm thrashing succeeded in getting the child to do anything more than cry.

Even when you succeed in using your physical force to coerce them into doing what you want, you may still be unable to control the child's thoughts, attitudes, and values. You may force your children to say "thank you" or "I'm sorry," but they will not necessarily feel grateful or sorrowful. You might succeed in forcing your children to attend church, but you can't make them like it.

(You can lead a horse to water, but you can't make it drink.) Rather than creating an impasse, parents and children are usually better off avoiding the impasse altogether. You should use patience and persistence to convey your standards of right and wrong and encourage your children to accept them.

## Spending Time Together

To build a close relationship, parents and children need to spend meaningful time together. Building a relationship requires time and effort — *both* quantity and quality time together. Just because you live under the same roof is no guarantee that you're going to build a close relationship. Busy fathers occasionally try to compensate for a lack of quantity by focusing on the quality of time they spend. "What good does it do," they ask, "to just sit watching a TV program together? That's hardly quality time. When we're watching TV we hardly even talk together."

While it is true that quality is an important consideration, most parents who use this excuse offer it as an inadequate excuse for not spending sufficient time with their children. Doing active, creative things and sharing personal feelings and insights are obviously superior to passively watching a TV program. But you need to assess both the quantity *and* the quality of the time you spend with your children. You should not assume that any amount of quality can compensate for quantity. Your children need to interact with you in a variety of situations, including quiet, thoughtful moments as well as intense, stimulating, and exciting times.

Some of the most meaningful activities parents and children can do together to build a close relationship involve talking about personal feelings and emotions or working together to create or build something. Sharing experiences that create happy memories is an important part of building a close relationship. Being able to share personal feelings and insights and knowing that you can confide your personal concerns and anxieties with each other is also important. Some activities need to be planned so that both parents and children look forward with joyful anticipation to the event. Other activities, however, need to be spontaneous so that some of the joy comes from the surprise and excitement.

## Co-opting Friends

When the relationship between you and your teenager is strained or severed, an effective way to begin rebuilding that relationship is through your child's friends. If you can become a friend to your children's friends, you will probably find the relationship between you and your children changing dramatically. This is called co-opting, or absorbing your child into your circle of friendship by absorbing his friends into your friendship. If you can succeed in building a friendship with your children's friends, you may also discover that your efforts are greatly appreciated by other parents. The following illustrations describe the success some parents have achieved in building a relationship with their children by co-opting their children's friends.

1. "By the time our son was seventeen, my husband and I decided we didn't even know him any more. He refused to talk to us; we didn't know what he was thinking. We had no idea who his friends were or how he spent his time.

"One afternoon a whole carload of kids came to our home and asked for our son. I told them he would be home in just a few minutes and invited them in. There was one fellow and four girls, and I sat in the living room and visited with them. They did most of the talking to each other, and I only tried to follow along in the conversation.

"One of the girls noticed a theater program of a Broadway play that my husband had attended when he was in New York. When I discovered her interest in Broadway plays, I realized we had something in common to discuss. She had collected the posters, scripts, and reviews of several Broadway plays, and I asked if she would let me look at them. I told her we had a book containing the musical scores from most of Rogers and Hammersteins productions, and she was anxious to borrow it. Over the next few weeks she and several of her friends made frequent visits to our home, and I soon felt that I had acquired some new young friends. At first we talked mostly about Broadway plays, but eventually we talked about other things, especially about school, dating, and other friends of our son. After a while I think our son actually began to feel jealous. I think he was afraid of being left out of a new social clique that was forming."

2.   "The best thing we did to establish a relationship with our daughter was to sponsor a surprise birthday party when she turned fifteen. We knew two of her friends and asked them if they would invite our daughter's ten closest friends to a surprise party. We picked up all of her friends in our van and arranged to have them surprise our daughter in the family room. Obviously our daughter was very surprised, and we had to wait twenty minutes for her to fix her hair.

"We had reserved one of the banquet rooms at the pizza parlor in an adjacent city, and we had a good opportunity to visit as we drove to the next city and ate pizza together. We sat around two large tables; my wife sat at one table and I sat at the other. We tried to just listen to the kids and get to know them a little better. It was  hard for us to relate to a few of them, but others were easy to get to know.

"I think it was good for our daughter to see some of her friends engaging in a meaningful conversation with her parents. I think that birthday party opened a lot of additional opportunities for us to get to know her friends and get closer to her."

3.   "I really had bitter feelings toward Scott, our son's best friend, even though I didn't know him well. He was the one responsible for most of the trouble our son had gotten into. I

finally realized, however, that if I was going to get close to our son, Rob, I would probably have to accept Scott.

"One day I saw Scott drive up in front and honk for Rob to come out. I slipped out the side door and walked around the front to make it seem like I had been outside all the time. I asked Scott if he wanted Rob, and when he nodded I walked to the front door and called, even though I knew Rob wasn't home. I then turned to Scott and asked him if he was in a hurry or if he could take a minute and help me move the picnic table to the other side of the house. He readily agreed to help, and then I began to wonder what kind of excuse I was going to fabricate to explain why we were moving the picnic table.

"As soon as he was on one side of the table and I was on the other, I told him the only thing I knew about the time he and Rob had tried to outrun the police was what I had read in the newspapers, since Rob never said anything about it. I concluded by saying, 'I suppose that must have been a frightening experience, wasn't it?'

"All he said was, 'Yeah, a little bit,' and nothing more was said until we discussed how far away from the house the picnic table should be placed.

"As we were getting the benches, I told him I was curious to know a little bit more about what happened that night, but he didn't immediately start to volunteer information. I asked for his advice about where we should relocate the swing set, and we discussed several possibilities. We talked about a few other trivial things like brown spots in the grass and defective sprinklers; but while we were moving the swing set, he finally started to tell me about their attempt to avoid a speeding ticket. He admitted that it was a dumb decision to try to outrun the police.

"I finally admitted that I didn't think Rob was home but suspected he would be there shortly, and as we sat and picked the dead leaves off some of the flowers I had my first opportunity to get to know Scott. I think he sensed my sincere desire to get to know him and accept him, and on several other occasions I was able to rely on Scott to help us convince Rob that what he was doing was wrong."

## Seconding Voices

According to *Robert's Rules of Order,* when a motion has been made, another person must second it before it can be debated and voted upon. Sometimes parents need a seconding motion to support and endorse their teachings. Parents expect other social institutions such as schools and churches to support them as they teach their children. Unfortunately, the schools do not always support parents as well as they should (and vice versa). Some social institutions, especially television, work at counter purposes to parents who want to raise socially responsible and morally clean youth. Therefore, to help you build a closer relationship with your children, you may find it advantageous to seek other seconding voices to support you.

Some of the best seconding voices come from the extended family, especially grandparents, uncles, and aunts. Seconding voices that come from non-relatives can also be very powerful. The mother of the third-baseman in a Pony League game called out to her son to tuck in his shirttail. The rules required that shirttails be tucked in, and the umpire refused to allow any batter to bat without first tucking in his shirttail. Her son knew the rule, but as he started for the dugout he looked up at his mother and shouted, "Hey, just shut up and forget it!" When he got to the dugout, his coach put his arm around his shoulder and tactfully told him that it was never appropriate to treat parents disrespectfully, and that even though he was the best batter on the team, he was going to have him sit on the bench for the next few innings and think about what he had done. Unfortunately, most coaches are more interested in their win-loss record than in the quality of young people they are developing. But this coach correctly understood that the most important thing he was developing was the character of young men and not just baseball skills.

Within the past three or four decades, the extended family has suffered enormously in our American society. Children today have much less exposure to their grandparents, aunts, and uncles than children had in earlier years. This change is very unfortunate in many ways, especially in raising children. Grandparents especially can be very effective in helping children learn right and wrong and internalize the values that their parents have been teaching them. Parents would do well to maintain a close relationship with their parents and demonstrate by the example of their own lives the kind of relationship parents should have with their children. The way parents treat grandparents will influence how their children will treat them in later years.

Since grandparents do not have as many natural opportunities to interact with their grandchildren today, parents need to make special efforts to create such opportunities. The kinds of opportunities that can be created are almost limitless, such as spending holidays together, eating Sunday dinners together, working in the yard together, going to the movies, or if the parents are far away, telephone calls, annual vacations, and pen pals. You may need to help grandparents remember important events, such as birthdays, school plays, band concerts, Boy Scout Courts of Honor, and other significant events when the children are recognized. Grandparents ought to either attend or at least extend congratulations.

You may also want to arrange opportunities for your children to interact with their uncles and aunts. The purpose of this interaction is not because Uncle Bill and Aunt Jane will say anything that Mom and Dad didn't say. In fact, they are likely to say the same thing, and it is because they say the same thing that this interaction is so beneficial. One possibility is to arrange for one or two-week stays for your children to live with an uncle or aunt. The children will discover that some things are quite different, such as the house, the furniture, the friends, and the food. But yet other important things are still the same, such as family prayer, obedience, self-discipline, and self-control. Although life may be different, certain fundamental values do not change.

## Pray Always and Keep Trying

Raising children can be very frustrating and disappointing at times because children are independent agents who can be expected to make mistakes. As parents, we all make mistakes, too. But rather than giving up in despair, parents should help children learn from their mistakes. Parent should not think of themselves as total failures every time their children do something wrong. They fail when they quit trying and abdicate their responsibility. Parents must pray always and keep trying.

It is not uncommon for parents to have some days when they feel fairly content that their children are progressing satisfactorily toward becoming responsible, mature adults and other days when they feel they are seriously failing. Personal development and maturity do not occur in a smooth, sequential fashion, and sometimes the rebelliousness that children display is caused by their struggles to become independent and to do things for themselves. Children are not required to go through a stage of rebelliousness and defiance; learning to be defiant is not a necessary part of maturing. But when teenagers become rebellious and defiant, parents should not think they have failed entirely or abandon their efforts to continue influencing their children.

After interviewing two thousand young men who decided to serve a mission for The Church of Jesus Christ of Latter-day Saints, I realized that at least a fourth of them reported that for a year or two during their teenage years they experienced a rebellious period. Some of them described only mild rebellion, such as refusing to talk to their parents, attend church, perform household chores, or get their hair cut. However, others described much more serious forms of rebellion, including substance abuse with alcohol, tobacco, and drugs; dropping out of school; and immoral or illegal behavior. Most of these young men admitted that they had worried their parents sick, and they weren't proud of what they had done. But after passing through a rebellious stage, they were anxious to do everything they could to put their lives back in order and behave as socially responsible adults.

Concerned parents feel devastated when one of their children rebels against God. These faithful parents often feel intense self condemnation and spend many anguished hours asking themselves what they did wrong and what they should have done differently. During these times of intense heartache, it is difficult to remember that children have their own personal agency and parents cannot deprive them of their right to make their own choices. Sometimes it is difficult for children to listen to the gentle encouragement of parents and the whispering of the Spirit when the sounds of the world are shouting at them from all directions. Elder Boyd K. Packer assures parents, however, that they should not despair:

"It is a great challenge to raise a family in the darkening mists of our moral environment. We emphasize that the greatest work you will do will be within the walls of your home, and that no other success can compensate for failure in the home. The measure of your success as parents, however, will not rest solely on how your children turn out. That judgment would be just only if we could raise our families in a perfectly moral environment, and that now is not possible.

"It is not uncommon for responsible parents to lose one of their children, for a time, to influences over which they have no control. They agonize over rebellious sons and daughters. They are puzzled over why they are so helpless when they have tried so hard to do what they should. It is my conviction that those wicked influences one day will be overruled....

"We cannot overemphasize the value of temple marriage, the binding ties of the sealing ordinance, and the standards of worthiness required of them. When parents keep the covenants they have made at the altar of the temple, their children will be forever bound to them."[44]

You should never abdicate your responsibility, abandon ship, or believe your situation is hopeless. Instead, you should constantly pray for your children and seek divine guidance to know what to do. Sincere prayers and dedicated efforts can help you establish a relationship with your children. The story of Alma in the Book of Mormon is an inspiring story illustrating the faith and dedication of a devoted father who was concerned about a wayward son. The angel who visited Alma the Younger expressly told him that he had come because of the prayers of his father and his father's people (see Mosiah 27:14). A few years later, Alma the Younger also had occasion to pray for the welfare of a wayward son (see Alma 39). We, too, should pray for our children, and they should hear our prayers and know of our concern for them.

## Securing Children Through the Everlasting Covenant

Parents who have been sealed in the temple and who suffer the heartache of seeing one of their children go astray can take great comfort in the teachings of several latter-day prophets. Brigham Young taught: "Let the father and mother, who are members of this Church and Kingdom, take a righteous course, and strive with all their might never to do wrong, but to do good all their lives; if they have one child or one hundred children, if they conduct themselves towards them as they should, binding them to the Lord by their faith and prayers, I care not where those children go, they are bound up to their parents by an everlasting tie, and no power of earth or hell can separate them from their parents in eternity; they will return again to the fountain from whence they sprang."[45]

Joseph Smith explained that the everlasting covenant could seal parents to their children: "When a seal is put upon the father and mother, it secures their posterity so that they cannot be lost but will be saved by virtue of the covenant of their father and mother."[46] Joseph Fielding Smith further explained that those born under the everlasting covenant are children of their parents throughout all eternity. "Nothing except the unpardonable sin, or sin unto death, can break this tie. If children do not sin as John says (1 John 5: 16-17), 'unto death,' the parents may still feel after them and eventually bring them back to them again."[47]    This promise is explained more fully by Orson F. Whitney:

"You parents of the willful and the wayward: Don't give them up. Don't cast them off. They are not utterly lost. The Shepherd will find his sheep. They were His before they were yours—long before He entrusted them to your care; and you cannot begin to love them as He loves them.... Our Heavenly Father is far more merciful, infinitely more charitable, than even the best of his servants, and the Everlasting Gospel is mightier in power to save than our narrow finite minds can comprehend.

"The Prophet Joseph Smith declared—and he never taught more comforting doctrine—that the eternal sealings of faithful parents and the divine promises made to them for valiant service in the cause of truth, would save not only themselves but likewise their posterity. Though some of the sheep may wander, the eye of the shepherd is upon them, and sooner or later they will feel the tentacles of divine providence reaching out after them and drawing them back to the fold. Either in this life or in the life to come, they will return. They will have to pay their debt to justice; they will suffer for their sins; and may tread a thorny path; but if it leads them at last, like the penitent Prodigal, to a loving and forgiving father's heart and home, the painful experience will not have been in vain. Pray for your careless and disobedient children; hold on to them with your faith. Hope on, trust on, till you see the salvation of God.

"Who are these straying sheep—these wayward sons and daughters? They are children of the Covenant, heirs to the promises, and have received, if baptized, the gift of the Holy Ghost, which makes manifest the things of God. Could all that go for naught?"[48]

In spite of its frustrations, raising children can be an extremely rewarding and meaningful accomplishment because it is part of a divine plan. From the beginning, mankind has been commanded to multiply and replenish the earth, which involves raising children and teaching them to be obedient and responsible. This commandment was not a curse, but a blessing. In the declining years of life, most grandparents agree that raising their children was the most significant and meaningful goal they accomplished, and they measure their happiness and success by the happiness and success of their grandchildren.

## Summary

*Building a meaningful relationship with children, especially teenagers, requires endless patience and persistence. Parents do not need to win each confrontation to succeed in teaching values.*

*Try to avoid win-lose confrontations; find alternatives where both sides may win.*

*Building a relationship takes time, both quantity and quality time.*

*Developing a relationship with your children's friends will help you build a relationship with your children.*

*By exposing children to other adults, especially grandparents, the influence of parents can be endorsed.*

*Parents should never abandon hope or cease striving to build a relationship with their children. Faithful parents who have been sealed by the everlasting covenant have the promise that their wayward children are still bound to them and this eternal seal will eventually bring them back again.*

# *Notes*

[1]A "Proclamation to the World issued by the First Presidency and Quorum of the Twelve Apostles." This proclamation was read by President Gordon B. Hinckley at the General Relief Society Meeting held September 23, 1995 in Salt Lake City, Utah.

[2]"Family Relations Manual." Published by The Church of Jesus Christ of Latter-day Saints (Salt Lake City, UT), 1987, Lesson 1.

[3]These three "degrees of glory" are described in the *Bible,* 1 Corinthians 15: 40 - 41, and in   Section 76 of *The Doctrine and Covenants*, Published by The Church of Jesus Christ of Latter-day Saints, Salt Lake City, UT, 1979.

[4]D&C 76: 82, 103-104. See versus 81 - 89 and 98 - 106.

[5]D&C 76: 72 - 75.  See versus 71 - 80.

[6]Alvin R. Dyer.  Quoted in "Family Relations Manual," Lesson 1.

[7]D&C 76: 79.

[8]Spencer W. Kimball, *Conference Reports*, April 1951, pp. 104-105.

[9]D&C 76: 51 - 53, 60, 69, 94.  See versus 50 - 70 and 92 - 96.

[10]*Book of Mormon*, 3 Nephi 12 - 14.

[11]Matthew 5: 3 - 12.

[12]  Matt 5: 22.

[13]  Matt 5:28.

[14]  Matt 5: 39-44.

[15]Matthew 5:20.

[16]D&C 121: 41 - 42.

[17]The research of Diana Baumrind is presented in four major publications:  Diana Baumrind, "Effects of Authoritative Parental Control on Child Behavior,"  *Child Development 37* (1966): 887-907;   Diana Baumrind, "Child Care Practices Anteceding Three Patterns of Pre-School Behavior," *Genetic Psychology Monographs 75* (1967): 43-88; Diana Baumrind, "Current Patterns of Parental Control," *Developmental Psychology Monographs 4* (1971, no. 1, part 2):  1-103;   and Diana

Baumrind and A. E. Black, "Socialization Practices Associated with Dimensions of Competencies in Pre-School Boys and Girls," *Child Development 38* (1967): 291-327.

[18]   Richard H. Blum and Associates, *Horatio Alger's Children* (San Francisco: Jossey-Bass Publishing Company, 1972).

[19] J. G. Friend and E. A. Haggard, "Work Adjustment in Relation to Family Background," *Applied Psychology Monographs* (1948, no. 16 whole), pp. 1-150; Melvin Kuhn and Donald F. Klein, "Social Values and Drug Use Among Psychiatric Patients," *American Journal of Psychiatry* 128 (1972): 131-33; Donald W. Goodwin, James Johnson, Chauncey Maher, Allan Rappaport, and Samuel B. Guze, "Why People Do Not Drink: A Study of Teetotalers," *Comprehensive Psychiatry 10* (1969): 209-14; John F. Kinnane and Martin W. Pable, "Family Background and Work Value Orientation," *Journal of Counseling Psychology 9* (1962): 320-25; Joseph C. Pentecoste, "Occupational Level and Perceptions of the World of Work in the Inner City," *Journal of Counseling Psychology 22* (1975): 437-39.

[20]Hugh Hartshorne and Mark May, *Studies in the Nature of Character Education*, vol. 1; *Studies in Deceit* (New York: The Macmillan Company, 1928): 369.

[21]   David J. Cherrington, *The Work Ethic: Working Values and Values That Work* (New York: AMACOM Publishing Company, 1980), chapter 7.

[22]Roland Keene, "Academic Achievement of Part-Time Workers at Southern Illinois University," Student Work Office, Southern Illinois University, December 1964: 1-39; John E. Hay, "How Part-Time Work Affects Academic Performance," *Journal of College Placement*, Vol. 29, No. 4 (April-May) 1969): 104; Jerry D. Augsburger, "An Analysis of Academic Performance of Working and Nonworking Students on Academic Probation at Northern Illinois University" *The Journal of Student Financial Aid*, Vol. 4, No. 2 (June 1974): 30-39; Ellen Greenberger and Laurence D. Steinberg, *When Teenagers Work: The Psychological and Social Costs of Adolescent Employment* (New York: Basic Books, 1986).

[23]Kerry Patterson, "Performance Skills For Managers: Problem Solving." (Interact Performance Systems, 1981).

[24]See the review by Martin L. Hoffman, "Child-Rearing Practices

and Moral Development: Generalizations From Empirical Research," *Child Development* 34 (1963): 295-318.

[25]S. Glueck and E. Glueck, *Unravelling Juvenile Delinquency* (Cambridge: Harvard University Press, 1950); William McCord, Joan McCord, and Alan Howard, "Familial Correlates of Aggression in Non-Delinquent Male Children," *Journal of Abnormal and Social Psychology* 62 (1961, no. 1): 79-93; Martin L. Hoffman and Herbert D. Saltzstein, "Parent Discipline and the Child's Moral Development," *Journal of Personality and Social Psychology* 5 (1967, no. 1): 45-57; W. Bromberg, *The Mold of Murder: A Psychiatric Study of Homicide* (New York: Grune and Stratton, 1961).

[26]Norma D. Feshback and Seymour Feshback, "Punishment: Parent Rites vs. Children's Rights," in G. P. Koocher, ed., *Children's Rights and the Mental Health Professions* (New York: John Wiley and Sons, 1976): 149-70.

[27]R. D. Parke, " The Role of Punishment in the Socialization Process," in R. A. Hoppe, G. A. Milton, and E. C. Simmels, eds., *Early Experiences and the Processes of Socialization* (New York: Academy Press, 1970). See other studies reviewed by Feshback and Feshback, "Punishment," and Hoffman, "Child-Rearing Practices and Moral Development."

[28]McCord, McCord, and Howard, "Familial Correlates of Aggression."

[29]W. McKinnon, "Violation of Prohibitions," in H. W. Murray, ed., *Exploration in Personality* (London: Oxford University Press, 1938): 491-501; J. Philippe Rushton, "Generosity in Children: Immediate and Long-Term Effects of Modeling, Preaching, and Moral Judgment," *Journal of Personality and Social Psychology* 31 (1975, no. 3): 459-66; Hugh Hartshorne and Mark May, *Studies in the Nature of Character Education*, vol. 1; *Studies in Deceit* (New York: The Macmillan Company, 1928).

[30]Martin L. Hoffman, "Moral Internalization, Parental Power, and the Nature of Parent-Child Interaction," *Developmental Psychology* 11 (1975, no. 2): 228-39.

[31]J. Philippe Rushton, "Socialization and the Altruistic Behavior of Children," *Psychological Bulletin* 83 (1976, no. 5): 898-913.

[32]McCord, McCord, and Howard, "Familial Correlates of Aggression."

[33]B. Mia Musanda Milebamne, "Perception des Attitudes et Pratiques Educatives du Peres par les Delinquants et les Normaux," *Canadian Psychiatric Association Journal* 20 (1975): 299-303.

[34] A.S. Neill, *Summerhill: A Radical Approach to Child Rearing* (New York: Hart Publishing Co., 1960).

[35] Harold H. Hart, ed., *Summerhill: For and Against* (New York: Hart Publishing Co., 1970).

[36] Haim, G. Ginot, *Between Parent and Child* (New York: Macmillan Company, 1965).

[37] Benjamin J. Spock, *Baby and Child Care* (New York: Pocketbooks, 1946, 1957, 1968, 1976

[38] James Dobson, *Dare to Discipline* (Wheaton, Ill.: Tyndale House Publishing, 1970).

[39]John Locke, "Some Thoughts on Education," (1690), in *The Works of John Locke in Nine Volumes*, 9th ed. (London, 1794), 8: 26-104; reprinted in Philip J. Greven, ed., *Child Rearing Concepts, 1628-1861* (Itasca, Ill.: F.E. Peacock Publishing, 1973): 18-41. The quotation is from page 20.

[40] John Locke, as quoted in Greven, p. 21.

[41] See Greven, *Child Rearing Concepts, 1628-1861*.

[42] John Witherspoon, "Letters on Education" (1797); reprinted in Greven, pp. 80-98. The quotation comes from page 89.

[43] John Locke, "Some thoughts on Education" (1690), as quoted in Greven, p. 26.

[44]Boyd K. Packer, *Conference Report*, April 1992, pp. 94-95.

[45]Brigham Young, *Journal of Discourses*, Vol 11, p. 215.

[46]Joseph Smith, *Teaching of the Prophet Joseph Smith*, p. 321.

[47]Joseph Fielding Smith, *Doctrines of Salvation*, Vol. 2, p. 90.

[48]Orson F. Whitney, *Conference Report*, April 1929, p. 110.

# *Index*

ability problems 124, 126
abortion 73
accidents 159
accountability 89, 97
agency, personal 92, 106, 115
aggressiveness 151, 154
Alma 200
anger 120
appreciation 98, 110, 115
arguments 32
Asian countries 78
assistance 94
athletics 158
aunts 196
authority 35, 164
   respect for 3 164, 165
avoiding impasses 190
basketball 118
Baumrind, Diana 42, 44, 50
beatitudes 23, 29
bed making 83
birthday party 194
blind obedience 42
Blum, Richard H. 47, 50, 176
body piercing 12
Bosnia 42
Boy Scouts 82, 117
Broadway plays 194
building relationships 186, 192
camp chores 53

celestial behavior 20, 22, 35, 37
chastity 60, 103
child abuse 181
child-rearing goals 48
child-rearing myths 41, 43
child-rearing practices
   authoritarian 44
   authoritative 45, 57
   effective 7, 8
   ineffective 4, 7
   lenient 15
   permissive 15, 40, 44
church attendance 50, 73
church callings 81
clipping a hedge 61
co-opting friends 193
commitment 91
compliance 62
confrontation 1
consequences 127, 129, 133
contingency management 105
conversation 35
criticism 31
dawdling 162
delegating assignments 89, 90
delinquency 43
describe the situation 120, 122
Deuteronomy 14
diagnosing problems 124

diligent worker 75, 77
discipline 72, 79, 175
discipline techniques
    induction 152, 154
    logical consequences
        144
    modeling 152, 154
    natural consequences 144
    power-assertive 149
    psychological punish-
        ment 148
    spanking 149
disobedience, causes of
    carelessness
        158
    curiosity 158
    forgetfulness 159
    laziness 162
    objectionable mannerisms
        161
    physical discomfort 157
    willful disobedience 163
divorce 73
Dobson, James 171
Doctrine and Covenants 15,
    18, 21, 22, 34, 178
drug use 47
Dyer, Alvin R. 22
dysfunctional families 36
Edwards, Jonathan 172
Eli 15
embezzlement 60
emergent problems 134, 141
emotion 154
engineering firm 88

environmental determinism
    107
Ephesians 179
everlasting covenant 200
Exodus 179
extinction 161
Fair Labor Standards Act 87
family chores 9, 48, 72, 79,
    81, 82, 91, 111
family environment 8, 19
family expectations 70, 79
family projects 7
family vacations 8
feedback 98
feeding the dog 138
firm discipline 4
fornication 56
freedom 46
freedom of choice 36
frugality 73, 79
gambling casino 114
garden 72, 82, 84
German prison camps 42
Ginott, Haim 170
gold stars 102
grades 104
grandparents 196
habit of saying no 180
happy families 28, 70
Hartshorne, Hugh 65
healthy families 19, 37
high-risk families 47
hippie attitudes 49
honesty 29, 103
honorable men 21

house cleaning 83
hypocrisy 28, 58, 60
identification 62
imitative behavior 58
immodest clothing 17
imposed consequences 129, 130, 132, 141, 165
induction 55
integrity 54
interactions 35
internalization 62-64
intrusive child-rearing 172
Japan 78
Jonestown 42
Kimball, Spencer W. 22
Law of Moses 25
listening 32
Locke, John 172, 185
love withdrawal 149
low-risk families 47
lying 56
marijuana 48
masturbation 56
Mather, Cotton 172
May, Mark 65
meaningful jobs 85, 99
modeling 55, 58, 153
money 102
moral importance of work 76
moral internalization 152
Mosiah 14
motivation problems 124, 125, 127-129
motives 35
mottos 57, 71, 72, 84

mouth noises 161
mowing lawns 117
music lessons 81
musical instruments 8
My Lai massacre 42
natural consequences 129, 132, 141, 159, 165
Neill, A. S. 168
nose picking 161
obedience 72, 79
outstanding workers 71-73
Packer, Boyd K. 199
parental approval 103
parental authority 178
parental control 43
parental expectations 59
parental influence 167
parental responsibility 10, 13, 14
part-time job 70, 88
patient 120, 186
peanut butter sandwich 39
permissiveness 43
personal choice 91
personal responsibility 73, 79, 81
personal worth 75, 77
Pharisees 27
piano practicing 136
pizza parlor 194
pornography 73
praise 98, 102
prayers 200
pride in craftsmanship 76
primary reinforcers 102

problem-solving skills 117,
    119, 126
Proclamation to the World 20
profanity 56
Proverbs 14, 57, 69, 168
providing resources 96
psychological contract 89
psychological punishment
    159, 165
punishment 106, 123
reasoning 149
rebelliousness 41, 42, 198
reciprocal determinism 107
recognition 102
reinforcement 98
reinforcers 106
religion 70, 72, 79
reward programs
    allowances 111
    job charts 113
    random rewards 114, 115
    tokens 112
rewarding good behavior
    109, 115
rewards 106
rich people 78
Robert's Rules of Order 196
Robinson, John 172
role-play episodes 135-140
Rousseau, Jean-Jacques 168
Samuel 15
sandwiching 121
sarcasm 30
schoolwork 81
Scribes 27

scriptures 56
secondary rewards 102, 115
seconding voices 196
self-control 70, 172
self-denial 73
self-discipline 172
self-esteem 177
self-reliant children 43
self-respect 177
selfishness 31
Sermon on the Mount 23
service projects 81
sexually active 48
Singapore 78
slot machines 114
Smith, Joseph 22, 200
Smith, Joseph Fielding 200
social approval 102, 115
social influence 35
social responsibility 10
spanking 149, 164, 177,
    182
Spock, Benjamin 171
sports 81
sprinkler 93
stealing 56
strict discipline 41, 42
strict obedience 57, 172
successful marriage 20
Summerhill 168
supervising work 89
survey of work values 70
swearing 33
Taiwan 78
teaching moment 65, 67, 68

teaching responsibility 9
teasing 139
teenage employment 87
telestial behavior 20, 28, 35,
    37
temper 179
temper tantrum 2, 3
tennis 107
terrestrial behavior 20-22, 26,
    35, 37
Timothy 14
twig 69
uncles 196
unpleasant jobs 86, 99
unproductive worker 75
valiant in the testimony of
    Jesus 22
value internalization 61
verbalize feelings 1
washing dishes 137
wayward children 201
Wesley, Susanna 172
Whitney, Orson F. 201
willful disobedience 151
win-lose situations 190
Witherspoon, John 172
work ethic 70
work values 69, 74
workaholic 77
yard work 70
Young, Brigham 200

# David J. Cherrington

David Cherrington was born in Grace, Idaho, and reared in nearby Preston. In high school he was active in music, football, and track.

He attended Utah State University, interrupting his formal education for an LDS mission to the eastern states. He graduated from Brigham Young University with a major in psychology and a minor in mathematics. At Indiana University he earned both his master's and doctor's degrees in business administration.

The author has taught at the University of Illinois, the University of Wisconsin—Madison, BYU–Hawaii Campus, and (for the University of Southern California) Malstrom Air Force Base. He is currently a professor of Organizational Leadership and Strategy at Brigham Young University and is the author of several major journal articles and textbooks on human resource management, organizational behavior, the work ethic, ethical decision making, and moral leadership.

David Cherrington is married to the former Marilyn Daines, and they have four children, all married, and three grandchildren. He and his wife reside in Orem, Utah.

Cover photograph by Brent Tobler